Journey to
Autonomy

Pastel portrait of Louise Rosenfield by C. V. A. Röling, 1932.

Journey to Autonomy

A MEMOIR

Louise Rosenfield Noun

Iowa State University Press   Ames

The author wishes to thank David Archie (*The Iowan*), Marjorie Nichols Hufnagel, David Penney, David Westphal (*Des Moines Register*), and Joan Liffring-Zug for permission to use their photographs in *Journey to Autonomy*.

Manufactured in the United States of America

⊚ This book is printed on acid-free paper.

Book designed by Joanne E. Kinney

First edition, 1990

Library of Congress Cataloging-in-Publication Data

Noun, Louise R.
  Journey to autonomy : a memoir / Louise Rosenfield Noun. — 1st ed.
    p.   cm.
  ISBN 0-8138-1899-0
  1. Noun, Louise R.   2. Feminists—Iowa—Biography.   3. Women
civic leaders—Iowa—Biography.   I. Title.
HQ1413.N68A3   1990
305.42'09777'092—dc20   90-4187

To Sally Hacker

CONTENTS

Journey to
Autonomy

1

FAMILY

People who know me today as a self-assured and assertive person are incredulous when I tell them that for a good portion of my life I was shy, insecure, and lacked self-esteem. I was often afraid to speak up in defense of my own opinions if, in fact, I really knew what my opinions were. I was motivated by a desire to conform and be accepted socially even though I might not wholeheartedly approve of situations in which I found myself. Why was I unable to come to terms with the various elements in my life? Probably much of this inability was due to my own nature. But looming large in the picture was my very strong but unloving mother.

Mother tried to do the right thing for her three children by seeing to it that we were well educated, well dressed, and well mannered but she unwittingly cowed us in the process. As far as I can recall, neither my sister, Ruth, my brother, Joe, nor I ever challenged Mother directly. My sister and brother were born two years apart and I came along four years later, in 1908. When I finally got the courage to ask, my mother readily admitted that I was an unplanned child. I suspect that I was not only unplanned but also unwanted. Mother made no secret of the fact that she almost died when I was born and that I made her suffer because I refused to nurse when her breasts were painfully full of milk. I was always stubborn, she said. Also, Mother never offered us any physical affection such as a friendly hug, nor was she the kind of person we went to for sympathetic understanding. We were strictly a "hands off" family and loath to reveal our personal feelings to one another. Praise for her children was not in Mother's nature and I grew up with a feeling of unworthiness. No matter what successes I had, I never felt fully accepted. Instead of physical punishment Mother gave what she called "tongue-lashings." I can recall my sister dissolving into tears after these harangues. I simply cowered. My brother was spared; he could do no wrong. My resistance came in oblique ways. Every night when I departed for bed I was expected to say "Goodnight, Mother" and "Goodnight, Father." I felt that such expressions should come spontaneously so I stuck to a plain "Goodnight." Night after night I was summoned back to say goodnight properly. Except in small ways, however, I never questioned my mother's authority until mid-life, when, with psychiatric help, I tried to come to terms with what her domination had meant for me. Since her death I have come to understand some of the frustrations in Mother's life and appreciate the many worthwhile values that she gave me.

My father, Meyer Rosenfield, was a quiet, shy person, rather short in stature, with thinning gray hair and rimless glasses. He was a partner in the Harris Emery Company, a department store on the site of the present Financial Center, which he owned with my mother's brothers. When I was in college this store was merged with Younkers. Father came home for lunch every day, unlike most of his colleagues who ate at the prestigious all-male Des Moines Club. At the time I was not aware that for a man to have lunch at home was an unusual practice, nor was I aware that Father refused to go to evening social events or entertain guests for dinner. His only evening recreation was to meet with my uncles several evenings a week at Grandmother's house, where they would discuss business. My brother, Joe, told me only recently that Mother once confided to him how depressed she was during her early married years because of Father's lack of sociability. Father's life was primarily directed to business and he let Mother run the show at home. He paid for all our living expenses, which left Mother free to use the income from her father's inheritance for charitable enterprises.

When I was little, Father used to read *Alice in Wonderland* to me, and I never tired of hearing the verse:

> "You are old, Father William," the young man said,
> And your hair has become very white;
> And yet you incessantly stand on your head—
> Do you think, at your age, it is right?"

"In my youth," Father William replied to his son,
"I feared it might injure the brain;
But now that I am perfectly sure I have none,
Why I do it again and again."

Father once spanked me, probably a unique occasion. When he finished I said to him, "You forgot to say 'excuse me.'" As we grew older Father paid very little attention to Ruth and me but he had a close relationship with my brother. My father died of cancer in 1929, at the age of sixty-four, when I was a senior in college. Mother lived on for another thirty-one years.

I never knew my Rosenfield grandparents and I can't remember Father ever talking about his parents or his youth, so I know very little about his family history. Since my brother, Joseph, is named after Grandfather Rosenfield, I am sure my grandfather was no longer living when Joe was born. It is Jewish custom never to name a child after a living relative. Both my Rosenfield grandparents came from Germany to the United States in the 1850s and settled in Rock Island, Illinois. My brother tells me that Grandfather Rosenfield, in contrast to many emigrants who left Europe to avoid military service, served two terms in the military before he left Germany. According to Joe, Grandfather liked his first army stint so well he signed up for a second. Grandfather owned a bank in Rock Island and I think he was also in the leather business. In those days selling harnesses to settlers going West and supplying leather equipment to the nearby Rock Island Arsenal was a lucrative occupation. All I know of my grandmother Rosenfield is that she gave birth to ten children, one of whom died when he was ten years old. Two of Father's sisters, Carrie Rosenfield Levy and Flora Rosenfield Strauss, lived in Creston, Iowa, where their husbands operated a clothing store. I can recall going to Creston to see them from time to time but I never knew them well. I have a more vivid memory of Father's two cousins, Stella Rosenfield Sax and Hattie Rosenfield Ettinger, who also grew up in Rock Island. Hattie lived in Osceola, Iowa, and Stella in Ottumwa, Iowa. Their husbands each owned a clothing store in their respective communities. Both women collected antiques and Mother had much more in common with them than with my father's sisters. In 1909 when Mother was looking for antiques for our new home on Thirty-seventh Street, Stella Sax, who was well acquainted with the New York antique market, met her in New York and helped her select several pieces of furniture, among them the big four-poster bed for our guest room which I was allowed to sleep in when I was sick. I can remember the double parlors in the Sax home in Ottumwa with their elaborately carved furniture made by the famous Victorian cabinetmaker John Henry Belter. When the Sax home was dismantled by their daughter in the early 1940s she gave the Belter furniture to the Des Moines Art Center, which was then in the planning stage. I helped her in making arrangements for this gift. The Art Center later loaned this furniture to Terrace Hill where it is now on display.

I know more about my mother's family than I do about the Rosenfields since I grew up surrounded by Frankels. My grandfather, Isaiah, was born in Ichenhausen, a village in Bavaria, in 1832. At age fourteen he was apprenticed to a cigarmaker and later he worked as a clerk. Isaiah came to the United States in 1853 when he was twenty-one years old. He first went to southeast Ohio and then to northern Missouri, and in 1861 he moved to Oskaloosa, Iowa, where he opened a small clothing store. He married my grandmother, Babette Sheuerman, in 1864. They had six children, two girls and four boys. As Isaiah prospered, he enlarged his clothing store and also opened a bank. A building on the Oskaloosa town square which Isaiah built in 1889 still carries the Frankel name. Isaiah served four terms on the Oskaloosa City Council and apparently was a highly respected citizen in Oskaloosa. He was a founding member of the Temple B'Nai Jeshurun, the reform Jewish congregation in Des Moines, which was organized in 1878. The three older Frankel sons, Ansel, Manass, and Nate, all went into business with Isaiah. In 1894 they opened a branch store in Des Moines. Henry, the youngest child in the family, was sixteen at the time of his father's death. He was the only one of the Frankel children to receive a college education. I cannot recall my mother saying very much about her father but I got the impression that he was a rather severe man. Mother did tell me once that he never gave his wife or children spending money but that he always bought whatever they needed. My brother Joe recalls that Isaiah required his sons to be at his store every day, including Sundays and evenings. At one point his son, Manass, rebelled and went across the square to work for a competitor. When Manass reported for work the second day, his boss said, "Your father has just been here and fired you." Isaiah died in 1897 from complications caused by diabetes. His obituary in the *Oskaloosa Herald* (April 2, 1897) says this of him: "While possessed of a considerable fortune his career has been free from speculation and his money has been made by energy, perseverance and good judgment. [He was] always generous to a fault, philanthropic without display, thoughtful of home and friends always, and above all an enemy to idleness. . . . Improvement was Mr. Frankel's hobby and the city owes much of its advancement to his work and advice."

I remember my grandmother, Babette Sheuerman Frankel, very well. She lived next door to us while I was growing up and I used to spend a good deal of time at her house. Babette was born in 1840 in Binau on the River Neckar, a small German village near Heidelberg. When my grandmother was in her eighties my mother persuaded her to write an account of her early life. Grandmother begins this account by saying, "The life of a child in the town where I was born is not so much a life of affairs as a pity that it has to be spent in such surroundings." Babette says she was not interested in school but always enjoyed being outdoors, turning hay in the fields of the local peasants or setting out plants. Often she did these things without her parents' permission. When she was very young, Babette earned money by ironing bosom shirts for her neighbors and making bread dough. She was so small that she had to stand on a stool to reach her work. "I was very handy and not like a child," she writes with pride, "and I was well paid." Babette left school when she was ten years old and joined her sisters, Rose and Sophie, ages twelve and a half and eight, in what Babette terms a millinery business. This business consisted of making the peasant caps worn by the local women and also serving as a laundry service: washing the caps (probably in the River Neckar) and ironing and ruffling them. Their business extended to all the neighboring villages and all deliveries were made on foot. Babette's job was to deliver finished goods and pick up new work. She carried her wares in a basket on her head. Sometimes she had to walk as long as four hours each way. When she was afraid going through the woods she would "run like a deer." One early spring day after an especially long trip she found that the ice on the River Neckar had broken up since she had crossed in the morning. She had to jump from one piece of ice to another in order to get back home.

In 1847 Babette's oldest brother, Abraham, came to the United States and settled in Muscatine, Iowa. Three years later her older sister, Rose, joined Abraham in Muscatine where she found work in a millinery store owned by a Mrs. White. After the death of her father in 1857 Babette, her sister, Sophie, her brother, Leopold, and their mother, Sarah Lipschutz Sheuerman, also came to the United States. Rose and Abraham sent them the money for this journey. They were too poor to pay for passage on a steamship so the family came on a sailing vessel which took thirty-six days to go from LeHavre to New York. They had to take all the provisions for the trip with them. These consisted of zweiback, smoked meat, and a few canned goods.

By the end of the journey their supply of food became very scanty. Babette did all the cooking for her family over an open fire in a kind of fireplace in which kettles hung on hooks. She writes that she often was burned, probably from the hot swinging kettles. Babette prides herself on the fact that she was one of only three passengers who did not get seasick. Her mother and sister could not get out of bed the whole trip. When this group arrived in Muscatine they settled in a house which had been prepared for them by Rose and Abraham. By this time Rose was the forewoman in the millinery store and Sophie and Babette went to work there. Their mother kept house for them. Abraham Sheuerman moved to Marengo, Iowa, in 1859 where he opened a small store. As soon as he was financially able to do so he brought Babette, Sophie, and Leopold to Marengo. (By this time Rose had married and was living in Elgin, Illinois.) Leopold was given a half interest in Abraham's business. About 1870 the Sheuerman brothers bought a woolen mill in Marengo which they operated until they moved to Des Moines in 1882. Here they established the Capitol City Woolen Mills, which Leopold's sons continued to operate until the Depression of the 1930s. The company slogan was "From Sheep to Shape."

In January 1864 Babette and my grandfather, Isaiah Frankel, were married in Davenport in a double ceremony with Babette's brother, Leopold, and his bride, Matilda Schwartz. The wedding ceremony was performed by a Protestant minister. There obviously was no rabbi in Davenport at this time. Babette and Isaiah had met in Chicago but there is no account of how or when this meeting took place. After their wedding they returned to Oskaloosa by stage-coach. Ansel, the first of Isaiah's and Babette's six children, was born the year of their marriage. My mother, Rose, one of two girls in the family, was born in 1873 and Henry, the youngest child, was born in 1881. Charles Needham, who grew up in Oskaloosa and played with the Frankel boys when he was a youngster, had this to say about Babette: "She was a busy, hard-working woman, but she was never too busy to tie a cut finger, feel us over for broken bones, and heal the hurts with a cookie or an apple. There was nothing too hard or too much trouble for Mrs. Frankel to do for her children. She was a kind, good woman and a grand, good mother. She stands out as about the nicest person I knew in that period of my life." (Written for the *Grinnell Register* on the occasion of Babette's eighty-fifth birthday in 1925.)

After my grandfather's death in 1897, Grandmother, my mother, and mother's brother, Henry, traveled in Europe for a year. As far as I can tell, this trip marked Grandmother's emancipation and for the next ten years she did a good deal of traveling. One of my childhood memories is a picture in Grandmother's photograph album of her riding a camel in Egypt when she was seventy years old. I thought this a remarkable feat. After Grandmother, my mother, and Henry returned from their year-long European journey, they settled in Des Moines where Grandmother's three older sons were now in business. In her later years my mother mentioned to me that Grandmother couldn't wait to get out of Oskaloosa and away from my grandfather's sister, Sophie, who had lived in the Frankel household for many years. This was the first time I had ever heard of Sophie Frankel and I found that neither my brother nor my sister knew of her existence. This seems strange as we were brought up with stories about Oskaloosa. Census and cemetery records confirm her existence. Sophie apparently was the maiden sister who lived with her brother's family out of necessity and was so disliked by the rest of the family that they simply willed her out of existence by their silence. It seems that Sophie was caught in the bind of so many nineteenth-century single women who were forced on the charity of relatives because they had no means of earning their own living.

When my grandmother was in her early seventies she broke her hip, and because there was no way of pinning bones in those days she could walk only with the aid of crutches the rest of her life. I recall her as a stalwart, white-haired matriarch sitting in a high-backed chair in her living room. Grandmother was a major supporter of Piney Woods, a school for black children near Jackson, Mississippi, which had a chorus called the Cotton Blossom Singers. Whenever Lawrence Jones, the school's director, came to Des Moines with this chorus, he would bring the singers to Grandmother's house for a private concert. I can recall attending at least one performance by this group in Grandmother's living room. I always felt warmly received in Grandmother's house and enjoyed playing pinochle with her. Once, when I was about six years old and vacationing with my parents in Colorado, Grandmother sent me a dime for being a good girl. A short time later the hotel in which we were staying burned to the ground. The only loss I have any memory of is Grandmother's dime. No doubt this particular loss was memorable because it represented a token of approval which was otherwise so lacking in my life. Grandmother was known as a good cook and her kuchen breakfasts were famous. On Sunday mornings my family and my uncles and aunts and their families would gather around Grandmother's table for a variety of those luscious open-faced pastries—apple, plum, peach, cherry,

poppy seed, even onion kuchen. What a treat! On hot summer evenings Grandmother's open terrace was a favorite family meeting
place. Here we would visit while we burned punk to keep the mos-
quitoes away, fanned ourselves with palm-leaf fans, and covered our
heads with towels when the bats swooped too low. Grandmother
never forgot the hardships of her early life in Germany and she was
always grateful for the opportunities which she found in this country.

Grandmother's family, the Sheuermans, were a numerous and
close-knit clan. There were fifty of us—cousins, uncles, aunts, parents, and grandparents—in Des Moines. Annual family gatherings,
usually picnics at Greenwood Park, were called "Neckar-Binaus" in
honor of the older generation's home in Germany. I can recall these
gatherings as happy affairs with much good food and songs composed by family members. In her old age Grandmother sent copies
of these songs to her brother Leopold's granddaughter, Mitzi
(Matilda) Jung, in Milwaukee. "You are the one of all the rest I will
trust with my treasures," Grandmother wrote. "Read them and keep
them as you can best." Grandmother's trust was well placed. Mitzi
did keep the songs and when I became interested in family history
she got them out of her attic for me to see. Here is a sample sung to
the tune of "America."

    Oh, Binau, 'Tis of thee,
    And of the Sheuerman tree,
    Of thee we sing!
    Aunt Sophie, we love you,
    To Uncle Lee we're true,
    And our Aunt Babette, too,
    Thy names we love!

    Let music swell the breeze,
    For we are the whole cheese,
    On this great day!
    We've come to Greenwood Park,
    To have an old time lark,
    We won't go home 'til dark,
    Neckar Binau!

I recall, especially, the Neckar-Binau party held in the Harris
Emery tearoom in December 1916 in honor of my grandmother and
my great uncle, Leopold. Relatives came from Milwaukee, Chicago,

Kansas City, and other communities to join in honoring these two. Old photographs were displayed and a very clever paper published for the event. This paper, the *Binau Blatt*, is full of good humor and comments about family members, such as the following poem dedicated to my father:

A woman's place is in the home
We all know that
But brave is the man
Who goes home each day
To lunch with his suffragette!

A column titled "At the Movies" lists, "Rose Rosenfield in 'The Weary Wife,'" which will play all week. This item reminds me that Mother did complain of being tired a good deal of the time.

My mother's sister, Henrietta Frankel Pfeifer (Aunt Ettie), lived with my grandmother. Aunt Ettie, a gentle, kindly person, was a widow whose husband, it was whispered, died of syphilis. She was very hard of hearing and wore a hearing aid attached to a large battery which she kept tucked in her bosom. She liked to garden and make appliqué quilts. In her later years Aunt Ettie was absorbed in collecting antique French fans and my trips to Europe always involved searching out additions for her collection. Three of my mother's brothers, Uncles Henry, Nate, and Ansel, lived within a short walking distance of Grandmother's house. The fourth, Uncle Manass, retired from business early and moved to Paris with his wife, May Burns Frankel. Aunt May was the daughter of an Irish policeman in New York and had worked as a manicurist before her marriage. Joe tells me Uncle Mannas sent May to a finishing school before bringing her to Des Moines but that she never felt comfortable living here. Aunt May was a Catholic and the first Christmas tree I ever saw was in her apartment after she came here as a bride. In later years I often heard Aunt May complain of Mother's uppity manner. Doubtless, Mother did not have any great love for May but she never said so. In fact, Mother never spoke ill of any near relative, hence I lost out on a lot of juicy family gossip. Aunt May had style and dressed beautifully in Paris couturier clothes. Once in a while I would inherit one of her cast-off dresses.

Mother's effect on people she did not care for was aptly described by her cousin, Selma Sheuerman Lyons of Kansas City, who reported that a visit with Rose Rosenfield sent chills up and down her spine. According to my cousin, Bert Strauss, who is my sister's age, Mother was considered "standoffish" by his parents. "This she was," he says, "having no time to waste on gossip." Bert describes Mother as forceful, highly intelligent, and interested in world affairs as well as in gardening, art, and antiques. She was the member of his mother's generation for whom he had the most respect. On the other hand, Bert's wife, Fritz (Frances), tells me that she always thought of Mother as the "gray eminence."

Mother had such a dominating personality that it is difficult for me to distance myself far enough from her commanding presence to give a very clear picture of her. She was dignified, fairly tall, and once had black, curly hair. I remember her best in her later years when she had short, gray hair and the stout figure typical of many women her generation. My daughter, Susan, after meeting Eleanor Roosevelt, commented that she looked just like Mother. Both women had the same type of figure but Mother was better looking. In fact, judging from photographs of Mother when she was young, she must have been quite beautiful. When I was in college Mother was in a bad automobile accident and the right side of her forehead was crushed. She carried the scars of this accident for the rest of her life. Mother liked to dress well but in a conservative manner. She never wore high-heeled shoes and her only makeup was a rice face powder which, if I remember correctly, was made by the LaBlage Company.

Mother grew up in Oskaloosa where she graduated from high school. She wanted to go to Vassar College, an unusual ambition for a woman of her day, but her father refused to send her. Instead, he let her go to the Loring School in Chicago for two years of post–high school work. This was an experience that she always cherished and she continued a friendship with members of the Loring family as long as they lived. Mother told me in her old age that she loved living in Oskaloosa until she went away to school. After that, Mother found this small town pretty confining. She thoroughly enjoyed her year-long trip to Europe in 1898 with her mother and her brother, Henry, and I am sure Mother would have liked to continue to travel but her marriage in 1900 to my father, who loved nothing better than to stay at home, put an end to any European journeys for the next twenty-five years.

My parents were married in Des Moines and they set up housekeeping in what is now known as the Sherman Hills area. In 1909, when I was a year old, they moved to a large Tudor-style home which they had built at 207 Thirty-seventh Street, south of Grand Avenue. This street was still a dirt road when we moved there, and because of its brown color, Grandmother dubbed it "Cinnamon Alley." All the property south of us on our side of Thirty-seventh Street was native woods. Just to the north of us was Grandmother's new house and across the street there were large homes recently built by Gardner Cowles, owner of the *Des Moines Register*, and Arthur Reynolds, a prominent banker. Half a block away was Greenwood Elementary School, which Ruth, Joe, and I all attended. The Thirty-seventh Street house was Mother's dream home and she stayed there as long as she lived. Her special joy was gardening and her large yard was a showplace of Des Moines. When she worked in her garden she wore an avant-garde suit consisting of khaki knickers and a matching, belted jacket. Ruth was embarrassed by Mother appearing in pants, even in the privacy of her own yard. I can't recall that I had either positive or negative reactions. Radical as this outfit might seem to others, if Mother chose to wear it, I would be the last to question its propriety. Mother was a staunch supporter of women's suffrage although when I asked her in later years if she had ever marched in a suffrage parade, she said she would never have had the courage to do it. She told me that in 1916 she gave $10,000 (which was a lot of money for that time) to the campaign for ratification of a woman suffrage amendment to the Iowa constitution. Her friend, Flora Dunlap, headed this effort. This amendment was rejected in an obviously fraudulent election but the women were powerless to do anything about it. My own memory of this campaign is Mother coming home from canvasing in the Roadside district of Des Moines, an area so poor that most homes did not even have running water, and reporting that one woman told her she didn't believe in suffrage for women, that a woman's place was in the home.

We children always took Mother's support of women's suffrage for granted, but her feminism was also evidenced in other ways which were not always appreciated or understood by us. She gave each of us her birth name, Frankel, for a middle name and we always considered this rather vain on her part. With my current feminist perspective, I now see this naming in a more sympathetic light. At that time it would have been impossibly radical for Mother to keep her birth name after marriage, but at least she could give it to her children. In the years when I was growing up the *Des Moines Tribune* gave an annual community award for outstanding citizenship. Mother resented the fact that this award almost invariably went to a man. In 1954 she decided to campaign for the award to be given to Ida Miller, a long-time teacher who prepared foreigners for their citizenship examinations. This decision was based on Mother's feminist principles, not friendship, for she had never met Miller. In addition,

my brother, who was active in community affairs, was also nomi-
nated for the award that year. Mother was determined that giving the
award to a woman was more important than giving it to her son. My
Uncle Henry, who was on the award committee, felt different. He
voted for Joe. I am not sure what Mother did to pursue her cause, but
it must have involved a lot of successful persuasion, for Miller was
given the award. This honor came to Miller when she was seriously
ill in the hospital and she died soon after. I thought Mother pretty
silly to make such an effort for a woman she didn't even know. This
was before I developed much of a feminist consciousness. Now I realize what a lonely cause it was for Mother to have pursued without
any peer support or even understanding on the part of her family. It
took dogged determination to achieve her goal. Had she lived long
enough, Mother would have found welcome cohorts in the current
women's movement.

One of Mother's long-term community interests was Roadside
Settlement, where she served as a board member and fund-raiser for
thirty-five years. This project was modeled after Hull House in Chicago, founded by Jane Addams. The purpose of settlement houses
was to have educated young men and women live in low-income,
usually immigrant, neighborhoods and work with their neighbors in
educational and economic-betterment projects. In addition to serving as a residence for the staff, settlement houses also served as community centers. Mother told me about going to Chicago in 1905 to
consult with Addams concerning a possible director for the Roadside
project. She recalled that she was awed by Addams who asked, "Do
you want someone to work for the poor, or with the poor?" It took a
truly strong person to impress my mother. On Addams's recommendation, Flora Dunlap, currently residing at Hull House, came to Des
Moines to head Roadside Settlement and she became Mother's best
friend. Over the years, Flora spent a great deal of time at our house
and seemed almost a member of our family. She was college educated and had enough money of her own to be economically independent. As I was growing up, I took Flora for granted, but as I look
back I can see what a remarkable person she was. She not only
headed Roadside Settlement, but she was a leader in many other
areas. She was the first woman to be elected to the Des Moines School
Board but announced she would not seek a second term because the
other board members—all males—ignored her at board meetings. In
addition to heading the campaign for woman suffrage in Iowa in
1916, Flora was active in organizing the Iowa League of Women Voters and served as its first president. She was also instrumental in

founding a Community Chest in Des Moines, the forerunner of the present United Way. Prior to funding by the Community Chest, Roadside Settlement was supported largely by funds collected annually by Mother and Flora from the Des Moines business community. I grew up with Mother's accounts of which men were generous and easy to approach and which were nasty and miserly.

Mother was also involved in founding the first Parent-Teacher Association in Des Moines, at West High School. This was accomplished in spite of the opposition of the superintendent of schools, who feared such an organization would diminish his authority. She ran the women's division of the war bond office during World War I and was the first to head the women's division of the Community Chest. (For many years the Community Chest and its successor, the United Way, had a women's division which solicited contributions house-to-house throughout the entire city.) Mother was appointed a charter member of the Des Moines Plan and Zoning Commission in 1926, serving on this body for two years. This job made her very aware of the lack of planning in Des Moines and I can remember her pointing out to me the plethora of dead-end streets as we drove around town. Being a woman on a board dominated by men was not always pleasant. She told me in later years how angry she once was with Jay N. Darling, the nationally known *Des Moines Register* cartoonist who was president of the Commission, when he took all the men on the board to dinner at the Des Moines Club while she was kept waiting an hour at the city hall for them to show up for a commission meeting. When the Des Moines Park Board was established in 1931 Mother was named a member. She served on this board a total of eight years, from 1931 to 1933, and again from 1937 to 1943. When the city received the Ewing farm as a bequest for park purposes, Mother conceived the idea of developing a lilac arboretum there and she persuaded the park board to go ahead with this project. She brought John C. Wister, a landscape designer from Swarthmore, Pennsylvania, to Des Moines at her own expense to consult about this project. Wister was subsequently hired to develop a long-range plan for the arboretum. Mother was a founder of the Des Moines Garden Club and later, when that club got too big, she helped found the smaller and more exclusive Founders' Garden Club. She was also interested in foreign affairs and in 1934 she endowed an annual lectureship in international relations in Father's memory at Grinnell College. Mother would have liked to have been fully integrated socially in the Des Moines community but there were barriers because she was Jewish. Many of her friends were members of Proteus, a small, exclusive study club, but she was never asked to join, doubt-less because of anti-Semitism.

When I was growing up Des Moines was considered more liberal than other communities because Jews were not barred from the Jun-ior League or the Des Moines Club. This was in contrast to Minneapo-lis where Jews were not even allowed to join the Automobile Association. Yet anti-Semitism, although much of it was covert, was pervasive. We tended to discount discrimination such as exclusion from two of the three country clubs in the city and from high school fraternities and sororities, partly, I think, because we were not will-ing to face further ostracism by complaining, and partly because we honestly believed that with time anti-Semitism would diminish. We had many gentile friends whom we considered tolerant and liberal people. If clubs they belonged to excluded us, it certainly was not their fault. We assumed that they had just inherited a bad situation that they would rectify when they had the opportunity to do so. Years later the bitter truth came to the surface when Wakonda Club members in 1961 reaffirmed the club's policy of excluding Jews as members. Even people whom we considered to be friends voted with the majority. The Holocaust had made me very aware that anti-Semitism should not be taken lightly. In the wake of the Wakonda sit-uation, I determined for the first time to speak out publicly on the issue. I wrote a letter that was published in the Sunday edition of the *Des Moines Register* a few days before Christmas protesting the Wakonda situation and suggesting that what was needed was the spirit of peace and goodwill. All that day I received telephone calls from members of the Jewish community thanking me for my letter. Calls from gentiles were few and far between. The one I remember vividly was from a German woman who worked as a waitress in pri-vate homes. She had known my father and wanted to commend me for my letter. "You can't believe what they are saying about the Jews at their dinner parties," she said. Fortunately today many of the bar-riers which Jews formerly faced in Des Moines have disappeared but I am fully aware of a continuing need to combat anti-Semitism along with all other forms of discrimination.

Although anti-Semitism added to Mother's frustrations in life, I believe her primary frustrations stemmed from her position as a woman in a sexist society. When she was without enough to keep her stimulated, she complained of being tired a good deal of the time, but given a challenging job she seemed to have plenty of energy. What Mother needed was the college education that she was denied, along with a career outlet of her own. In today's world she might have been a legislator, a journalist, or an art critic. As it was, most of her civic work was confined to unprestigious volunteer jobs considered suitable for women, and when she did serve on city commissions, she was in a subservient position relative to the controlling male power structure. As a result, Ruth and I became surrogates to fulfill Mother's dreams, regardless of how unsuited these dreams might be to our own interests and abilities. (Joe, of course, was destined for the business world.) Ruth, who was to have a career in politics, was sent to Vassar when she would much rather have gone to school in Iowa. After finishing at Vassar she was sent to Columbia University in New York City for postgraduate work in political science. Ruth dropped out of Columbia before completing the first semester. No one ever said why and I never thought to ask. I assume she either flunked out or found the work uncongenial. Meanwhile, when I was very young, Mother registered me at both Wellesley and Vassar and selected me to pursue a career in the art world, despite the fact that I showed no abilities or natural interest in this direction.

2

GROWING UP

My parent's house on Thirty-seventh Street forms a background for most of my youthful memories. It had a spacious, two-story front hall, a large living room, a dining room where Mother's collection of old pewter was displayed on a plate rail above the mahogany paneling, as well as a large solarium which was chilly in winter but provided a perfect climate for Mother's plants and flowering bulbs. With the exception of the solarium the first floor tended to be somewhat dark and somber. There were bookcases at one end of the living room on which stood bronze replicas of Roman sculptures that Mother had purchased in Italy. In the bookcases were sets of Jane Austen, Charles Dickens, William Shakespeare, John Ruskin, and other well-known authors. Mother gave me twenty-five cents for each book I read, but when she noticed that I was making money by reading a lot of short books, she reduced the price to ten cents for small volumes. At the other end of the room was an Italian refectory table on which current periodicals were placed. These included *Harper's*, the *Atlantic*, the *New Republic*, the *Nation*, *Foreign Affairs*, and in later years the weekly edition of the *Manchester Guardian*. The music room was so named because it housed the piano. I once had a few piano lessons from Edith Usry, a friend of Mother's, but these ended when Mother said that if I didn't practice I couldn't have any more lessons. This was fine with me. Apparently Edith didn't mind losing me as a pupil. When she died in 1975, Edith willed her entire estate, amounting to about $230,000, to the Des Moines Art Center for the purchase of works of art with the provision that nothing "commonly considered modern" be acquired with her funds. She named me in her will to see that her wishes were carried out. Her funds were used to purchase a still life by John Frederick Peto and a portrait of the Pailleron children by John Singer Sargent.

The dining room was always the scene for our family dinner, served by Rose Koeger, our German-born "second maid" who also did the dusting and cleaning in the house. Meals were prepared by Clara Berry, of Swedish background, who came from a farm in southern Iowa. Both Clara and Rosie worked for Mother for over thirty years but there was an enmity between them which prevented any friendly communication. All instructions as to guests for dinner, for example, had to be give to each woman individually because they were not likely to inform each other about setting another place at the table or preparing extra food. No one instance caused this incompatibility; it was just a difference in temperament. Rosie was high-strung and excitable and had trouble relating to people in general. Clara was even-tempered and seemingly easy to get along with although I suspect she had a stubborn streak when it came to making an effort to get along with Rosie. Clara loved to garden and was a great help in the yard. The kitchen was furnished only with a stove, a sink, and a fireless cooker, a contraption for slow, overnight cooking of food. A pantry with cupboards and an icebox adjoined the kitchen. Between the kitchen and the dining room was Rosie's domain, the "butler's" pantry with a sink for washing dishes and cupboards and drawers for storing silverware and china. There was also a maid's dining room adjoining the kitchen with a gateleg table and chairs with rush seats. A cabinet in the maid's dining room held Mother's collection of containers for flower arrangements. I usually had lunch in the maid's dining room. There the atmosphere was much more relaxed than at dinner with my parents, where we children were admonished not to put our elbows on the table or to use a piece of bread for a pusher.

Clara had a sister, Rose, who was our nursemaid when I was very small. She left to get married when I was about five years old and Clara came to work for us soon after her departure. I was heartbroken when Rose left because she provided much-needed warmth in my life. I am told that I kept saying, "Rosie and I are going to marry Sander Smith." I do recall sitting on the back stairs near our back door and watching Rose depart. A highlight of my childhood were visits to Rose's farm where I delighted in gathering eggs and going fishing with her husband, Sander, in the creek which ran through their property. Several years before she died Clara gave me a Christmas cactus that was found on the porch of Rose's farm home after her death. This cactus, which is still thriving, is a living memory of the Berry family.

My bedroom on the second floor of our house opened onto a large unheated screened porch were we children slept the year around. When we were growing up sleeping in the open air was considered very healthful. This porch was a delightful place in summer where there was usually a breeze even on the hottest nights. I can recall lying in bed at night and listening to the rumble of the trains as they ran across the valley about a mile below our house. They brought dreams of far-off places. In winter we had flannel sheets and the beds were warmed with copper warming pans—oval containers about twelve inches long and four inches high, filled with boiling water. A screw top secured the hole through which the water was poured. It wasn't so bad getting into bed in cold weather, but getting up in the morning was pure torture. Mother's way of getting me up was to tell me that my bath water was running and the tub would overflow if I didn't get up and turn it off. I never had the nerve to challenge her by just staying in bed. Besides being a throughway to the sleeping porch, my room also opened onto a bathroom that was connected to my parents' room. The result was that there was not much privacy in my domain. The guestroom with the antique four-poster bed was at the back of the second floor. When we were ill, we were usually put to bed there. I loved the relative isolation, the big bed, and the extra attention I got at such times.

Clara and Rosie each had a room on the third floor, and I often went up to Clara's room for a friendly chat. There was also a large playroom with a fireplace on the third floor that we decorated with red and green paper streamers for Christmas and where we hung our stockings for Santa Claus. However, we were not allowed to have a Christmas tree, a fine distinction that I could never understand. In later years the playroom was given to my sister for her bedroom. I envied her the privacy that she had there. Also on the third floor was a sewing room with a Singer sewing machine operated by a foot pedal. Every spring and fall a "sewing woman" would come for several days to shorten or lengthen our dresses as the styles of the moment dictated and, in general, to put our wardrobes in order. An unheated room on the third floor was a storeroom where we kept our luggage. Mother kept one wardrobe trunk in which to store memorable dresses, such as the one she wore for her wedding. From time to time Ruth and I would add a favorite dress to the collection in this trunk. I can remember, especially, a gold lamé evening dress which Aunt

May had given me. It had a daringly short, pleated skirt and a sleeveless, unbelted top. It was the height of style in the 1920s.

In addition to Clara and Rosie we had Frida Pearson, a husky German woman who came each week to do our laundry. I enjoyed going down to the basement and "working" with Frida doing handkerchiefs with my child-sized iron which was heated on a coal-burning range along with the irons Frida used. I recall Frida telling me this was good practice in case I might have to earn my living this way. I refrained from saying that I couldn't imagine such a dire situation.

We had a yardman who lived with his wife in an apartment over the three-car garage at the back of our property and also a driver whose services we shared with my grandmother next door. (The present attached garage and pool house were built by another owner.) We could call the garage or my grandmother's house through a primitive house phone system. These phones had buttons numbered one, two, and three. If I pushed the right combination of buttons the phone would ring at both Grandmother's house and the garage. Then I would listen with guilty delight as the person at each end of the line would try to find out who was calling whom. In the early days we also shared a car with Grandmother. This car was a Lozier limousine which had two tops—an open one for summer and a closed one for winter—which were changed with the seasons. The Lozier also had two folding seats which were always assigned to us children. Mother loved to go for drives in the country and the whole family would be taken on these expeditions. Mother would enthuse about the views as we went along and urge us to be equally enthusiastic. On the whole, we were quite uncooperative. I grew to hate these drives and as a teenager I would sit quietly and escape into a dream world far away from the Iowa countryside, in which I was a beautiful young woman much sought after by handsome young men.

At the far end of our yard was a cow barn where we kept two cows that supplied milk for our family. For a while we also had a pony that Ruth used to ride. Joe had trouble managing the pony and his riding career ended when he was tossed off and stepped on one day. I remember with horror Joe's friend, Arthur Reynolds, Jr., galloping up our driveway on his pony and calling to Mother that Joe had just been killed. Joe, who was scared but very much alive, was brought home and put to bed in the guest room. Dr. James Priestly, the family physician, looked him over and said there were no broken bones. I was considered too young and too small to even try to ride the pony. In later years my parents built a tennis court which provided a neighborhood gathering place until the Cowles built a bigger and better one behind their home down the street. Ruth and Joe were fairly good players. Struggle as I might, I never was any good at the game. My friend, Allen Brown, who was trying to help me with my game, told me one day, "Louise, don't try so hard. You are just not naturally athletic." In fact Mother considered me so awkward that she sent me to dancing school to acquire some grace. To add to my discomfort at not being any good at dancing, Mother refused to let me be in the annual dance recitals because she thought they were a waste of time and a needless display. Thus, I lost out on the fun of fancy costumes as well as the attention of my teacher, who wasn't interested in a pupil whom she couldn't show off.

Outside of the tennis court, Mother was loath to have us use her yard for recreational purposes in spite of the fact that our house was located on two acres of land. She didn't want her landscaping spoiled by worn grass or damage to her flower gardens. When I wanted to garden, she suggested digging wildflowers from the nearby woods and planting them under the shrubbery or in the ravine where they would be out of the way. Joe and his friends were always sent to the schoolyard to play ball, and our sandbox and playhouse were in Grandmother's yard next door. I was a strange child in that I liked to eat sand. I would also eat plaster that I picked off the sleeping porch wall. I have no idea why, except that it may have been an urge for self-destruction. Mother, who could never understand her children's actions in psychological terms, finally decided that this strange appetite was because I needed more lime in my system. At any rate the sand and the plaster seemed to have done no harm to my physical well-being.

I started going to Greenwood kindergarten at the age of four but was unable to stay awake in the afternoon so I dropped out. When I was five I entered kindergarten once again and I stayed at Greenwood until graduating from the eighth grade at the age of thirteen. Nellie Warren, a warm, friendly person, was principal of Greenwood. Once I was sent to her office for a misdemeanor. I went with fear and trembling but was confounded when Miss Warren looked at me and said with amazement, "What are you doing here?" No punishment was meted out, and in a way, I felt almost cheated. As I progressed, I skipped two half-grades and I always had a feeling that these promotions were due to pressure on the school authorities by my mother rather than to my own abilities. I have no evidence that this is true. What certainly must have been due to my mother's influence is my taking manual training instead of sewing and cooking.

I never would have thought of such a course on my own. One of our class projects was making birdhouses to enter in the *Des Moines Tribune*'s annual birdhouse contest. My birdhouse was not as well made as I thought it should be, so I covered it with birchbark to hide its defects. It looked so handsome that I won a prize. I felt that perhaps I had cheated and didn't deserve the honor. In promoting the contest the *Des Moines Tribune* ran a front-page picture of me and the two other girls in my manual training class with the heading, "Girls Make Birdhouses Too" (April 6, 1920). A certificate of merit, which Mother saved, attests to the fact that in 1920 I was recognized for excellence in English composition in a citywide contest but I have no memory of receiving this award.

When I was about eleven I went to a camp in northern Wisconsin for the last four weeks of its summer session. I had two cousins who were campers there so I did not feel like a complete stranger. When I said I would like to go on a canoe trip I was told that if I could demonstrate my swimming ability I would be eligible for a trip. I had no trouble passing the swimming test so off I went for a three-day jaunt. No one bothered to ask me beforehand if I knew how to handle a canoe. I sat in the bottom of the boat the first morning while other campers paddled. When I was asked to take my turn at paddling, I said I had never been in a canoe before and didn't know how to paddle. Thus, I remained a relaxed passenger for the entire trip. The camp as a whole must have been run in a similar slipshod manner because when Mother came to visit she decided not to send me back the following summer, despite the fact that I would have been perfectly content to go there again.

The next year Mother sent me to a camp in Maine where I knew no one while the rest of the family went to Glacier National Park. I left for camp in a brand new traveling outfit in which I felt very well dressed. It consisted of a navy skirt buttoned onto a white waist, white socks, low-heeled shoes, and best of all, a wide-brimmed navy straw hat decorated with streamers of embroidered ribbons. When I got to Chicago and met other girls going to the same camp I was completely taken aback. They were wearing heels, silk stockings, girdles, and sophisticated hairdos. I was the unsophisticated girl from the country and completely out of place. Camp was no better. The rest of the campers were sophisticates from New York and Washington with whom I had little in common. I didn't develop a single friendship and I felt like an outsider all summer long. If I hadn't been such a stoic I probably would have succumbed to homesickness. In contrast to the easygoing management of the Wisconsin camp, this camp was highly organized and competitive but I was such a poor athlete that the only award I won was for my efforts to improve my swimming and diving. All in all, it was the most miserable summer I ever spent. Determined not to appear again in my hat on the way home, I packed it in my trunk and substituted a beret that I had purchased in a nearby village. I was somewhat apprehensive as to what Mother would say when she met me, but she never even noticed my change of headgear. In my college years at Wellesley, I took a course in creative writing—not because I was interested in creative writing but because I needed some credits in English. For one of my assignments I wrote a story based on this camp experience that the professor, without revealing my name, read to the class with the comment that the author showed a lot of ability but, of course, would need much more experience before she could succeed. The idea of becoming a writer had never occurred to me and I dismissed this praise as an aberration. However, I never forgot it and in later years when I became serious about writing, I have often thought of this professor. Unfortunately, I can't even remember her name.

My first two years in high school were spent at West High School in Des Moines, which was located about two and a half miles from our house. The school was on the edge of a black neighborhood but it was not until years later that I came to realize that the so-called "intelligence tests" with which we were classified were a subtle means of segregation. As far as I can recall I only came into contact with black students in my gymnasium classes. Because the school was so crowded, students only attended half days. During my freshman year I went in the morning and the next year in the afternoon. Our driver would take me and some of my friends to school and after school we would walk to the car line and take the streetcar home. Recently, when I was telling my friend, Dan Johnston, about how I got to school, he commented, "Weren't you embarrassed about having a chauffeur take you to school?" I suddenly realized that I had never thought that other people might have considered me privileged. I simply took all our material advantages for granted and never gave any serious thought to other people's economic status. In fact, as a person with little self-esteem I never felt privileged, though in material ways I certainly was. Writing these memoirs about my youth has made me realize for the first time how very different my family's way of living must have been from that of many other people. As I think about it, I was far from alone in my indifference to issues of class and race. When I was growing up, black people in Des Moines were refused service in restaurants, made to sit in the balconies of movie theaters, and driven away from swimming pools used by whites despite the fact that all this was against the law. Although the community at large was aware of this kind of discrimination, it was accepted as one of the facts of life in Des Moines, even by those who deplored it.

I spent my junior and senior years at the newly completed Roosevelt High School. For the most part, my memory of these years is of being a painfully shy teenager who was never noticed by the boys and whose girl friends, for the most part, belonged to sororities which I was not asked to join. It was no secret that these groups did not take Jewish members. There were too few Jewish girls at Roosevelt to form a club of our own and even if there had been I doubt if I would have joined. Mother's ambition for us was assimilation, not segregation. Some friends of mine whose parents did not believe in sororities and fraternities went to Christian Endeavor meetings at Greenwood Congregational Church on Sunday evenings. I attended one meeting and the program consisted of singing hymns—or was it Christmas carols?—to the prisoners at the city jail. I found singing before men in cages very embarrassing. This cured me of Christian Endeavor. Betty Friedan, author of *The Feminine Mystique,* tells of her unhappy high school days in Peoria, Illinois, because of the anti-Jewish feeling that prevailed in the sororities and fraternities there. Although she would much rather have been part of the "in" crowd, she points out that being an outsider gave her "the power of observation—the social consciousness of an outsider."* I certainly find this true in my case.

In 1922, after my freshman year in high school, I went to Europe with my parents, my brother and sister, and my uncle Ansel, a widower, and his three children, Helen, Edward, and Ansel, Jr. There were nine of us in all with twenty-two pieces of hand baggage and also a few wardrobe trunks. Mother ran the show, planning our itinerary and deciding which sights we should see in each place we visited. We called Mother Mrs. Thomas Cook (Thomas Cook & Sons was a well-known travel agency). This was Mother's first trip to Europe since 1897 when she had gone with her mother. I couldn't get over the fact that it was twenty-five years since she had been abroad. That seemed an incomprehensible length of time to me. We sailed for France in June after attending my sister's graduation from Vassar, and Helen Frankel's graduation from Wellesley. Mother, using *Baedeker* as a guidebook, took us to every important historical monument in places we visited and I was an eager sightseer. In Paris I was

*Jennifer Moses, "She's Changed Our Lives," *Present Tense* 15, no. 4. (May/June 1988) 30.

impressed with the Greek sculpture, *Winged Victory*, in the Louvre and the magnificence of Napoleon's tomb in the Pantheon. I was puzzled, however, about why Napoleon deserved such an elaborate monument when he had led the French into so many wars. In Belgium we visited the site of the battle of Waterloo, which I found boring. Not in *Baedeker* were the World War I battlefields that we visited north of Paris. These were desolated areas with miles of trenches. They did little, however, to help me understand the horror of that war. I found much more meaning in the red poppies in the fields of the French countryside. These reminded me of John McCrae's popular poem about the war which begins,

> In Flanders' field the poppies blow
> Between the crosses, row on row that mark our place;
> And in the sky the larks, still bravely singing fly.

I was disturbed about the allied soldiers in Germany who were occupying the Ruhr and felt that their presence was sowing the seeds of future conflict. We went to Oberammergau to see the passion play, which I found very long and tiresome. What I remember best about our stay there was that the small hotel where we had paid for rooms beforehand was overbooked and some of us were put in rooms in private homes. I was with Uncle Ansel when he went to the desk clerk and demanded that he give us the rooms we had paid for or return our money. The clerk, with more customers than he knew what to do with, was more than willing to give back our money and he asked that we vacate our rooms. Uncle Ansel quickly retreated and for the rest of the day we didn't dare go out of the hotel without leaving someone behind to guard our quarters. Germany at this time was suffering from runaway inflation. I can recall waiting in a car outside a bank while Father went in to change some money. When he came out he was followed by a man with an armload of bundles of marks which were so bulky that the only place to put them was on the floor of the car.

In Germany, we went to Stuttgart to visit Rosenfield relatives. Father issued a blanket invitation to all his cousins to come to dinner and over thirty showed up. He had no idea who they all were. We were charmed with our Frankel relatives in Munich, who had a prosperous clothing manufacturing business and lived in tasteful and very beautiful homes. Less than twenty years later these same cousins were refugees from Hitler's Germany, and some were guests of my mother's in Des Moines. We went to my grandmother Frankel's hometown of Binau and I was horrified to see in the cemetery there graves of relatives who had been killed in pogroms. They seemed like the remnant of a dark age long past.

The male members of our party, with the exception of my father, went home in the early fall. The rest of us stayed on until late October and apparently no one, including me, ever worried about how I was to catch up with my schoolwork. We went to Monte Carlo, which is memorable because, being under age for the casino I had to stay in the hotel while my parents and Helen and Ruth went to gamble. In Italy we were surprised by men in black shirts who seemed to be in charge of our train going to Venice. We learned later that they belonged to a faction whose leader was a man named Mussolini. We had no idea of the significance of this event. We returned home late in the fall of 1922 and Mother made arrangements for tutors to help me make up the schoolwork which I had missed. One teacher, Miss Ogden, who taught modern history, balked at the idea of taking me into her class in the middle of the semester. She let me come in on a trial basis and I was soon her favorite pupil because of my knowledge of and enthusiasm for history which had been engendered by my European trip. I can't remember having any problems catching up with the rest of my schoolwork, which probably says as much about the poor quality of the academic program in high school as it does about my own intellectual abilities.

One of my most memorable family trips was to Banff and Lake Louise and then on to Alaska in the summer of 1924. We went down the Yukon as far as the ghost town of Dawson City on a wood-burning, paddle-wheeled boat which stopped several times a day to pick up fuel. The boat had no bathing facilities and there was only one bathtub in the old hotel in Dawson City. So all the passengers drew numbers and sat in the hotel lobby waiting their turn to use this tub. At that time Alaska was almost completely undeveloped as a tourist attraction and hotel accommodations were makeshift. In Skagway we went to a hotel (a remodeled store building) which Mother had heard had private bathrooms. The desk clerk assured her that each room had a bath so we decided to stay there. The clerk was technically correct. There was a bathtub in the corner of each room but all other facilities were down the hall! Alaska at that time still had many settlers with tales of the gold rush days. My brother's roommate on the river boat claimed to be the music boy in the *Shooting of Dan McGrew*, Robert Service's famous ballad about gold rush days in the Yukon. In Dawson I met a girl who had never seen a railroad. I thought this remarkable. Joe wanted to bring a husky dog home but Mother nixed that idea. All in all, Joe and I remember the Alaska venture as the best family trip we ever took.

During my grade-school and high-school years, Mother tried to groom me to be the artist she had always wanted to be, and she persisted despite the fact that I showed no ability or interest in this direction. When I was in elementary school she sent me to the Cumming School of Art on Saturday mornings. This school, located on the third floor of the public library, was run by Professor Charles Cumming who had studied at the Academie Julien in Paris. He came to Des Moines in 1895 to take over a struggling art academy and, when the Des Moines Public Library was completed eight years later, Cumming made a deal with the library to operate his school rent free in exchange for scholarships for indigent students. Cumming was obsessed with the threat to "culture" from African sources as evidenced in avant-garde painting in Paris and he was a vocal crusader for what he called the "white man's art." My personal memory of Professor Cumming is vague, as my contacts at the school were with Alice McKee (who was to become Cumming's second wife) and other assistants. I recall trudging up the steep steps to get to the school, the skeleton that hung by the entranceway, and the easel at which I labored at a charcoal sketch of a still life of bittersweet and copper kettles. I was smart enough to know that what I was producing had no merit but not independent enough to ever think of rebelling at these lessons. I have no idea how long I attended the Cumming school. It could have been one or more years. I recently came across an entry in the Des Moines City Directory of 1917 which, in listing my family, identifies me as a student at the Cumming School. Mother must have been sufficiently proud of this identification to give the information to the directory.

During my freshman and sophomore years in high school, Mother sent me to learn sculpture from Florence Sprague, a Des Moines artist teaching at Drake University. When I was younger, Mother commissioned Sprague to model a portrait head of me and I can recall sitting for her on the terrace of our home on Thirty-seventh Street. This project was eventually abandoned but apparently with no ill will on the part of either Mother or Sprague. Although I was officially enrolled as a Drake student, my lessons with Sprague were in fact private. I enjoyed them more than those at the Cumming School because playing with clay was more fun than working with charcoal. When I applied for admission to the Drake Law School many years later, I was amazed to find that I had been given credit for this work and that I earned high grades. I can't imagine why Sprague was so generous in grading a thirteen-year-old for I certainly accomplished little. My chef d'oeuvres were a full-length figure of Dante about ten inches high copied from a cast in the studio, and a crouching rabbit for which a live animal was the model. I helped cast both these pieces in plaster and then painted them. Neither showed any imagination or facility. Mother put them on a ledge in the solarium for a while. Eventually they found their way to the third floor where Rosie kept them on her dresser top as long as she lived in our home.

The pressures for me to become an artist were not confined to art lessons alone. In addition, I can recall birthday and Christmas presents of modeling tools and clay; a wood box containing oil paints, brushes, and palette; an easel; and a large box of pastels with a myriad of colors. I can't remember using any of these—not that I consciously rejected them, just that I did not have the skill to use them. There were also small reproductions of old master paintings to pin up in my room. This constant, though wordless pushing toward a goal for which I had little interest and no talent must have added to the feeling of inadequacy which dogged me well into adult life.

Along with her efforts to make me an artist, Mother encouraged me to become an art collector. For my thirteenth birthday she gave me an oil painting of a church in the Touraine by Harry Lachman, an American Impressionist. This painting was in an exhibition of Lachman's work sponsored by the Des Moines Association of Fine Arts that was on display at the public library. I remember going to the exhibition with Mother, and, at her suggestion, selecting the painting which I would like to have. I can't recall that I was thrilled with this present; on the other hand, it never occurred to me to suggest that there might be other things I might have wanted. Several years ago I was amused to find a 1921 clipping (*Des Moines Register*, March 6, 1921) in a file at the Public Library that announced that Mrs. Rosenfield had purchased a Lachman oil for her daughter, Louise, "who has developed a great interest in real art." In fact, the "great interest in real art" was my mother's, not mine.

Sometime during my high school years Mother became acquainted with a print dealer in Baltimore by the name of Cazdelbo. At her request, he would send prints from which I was to make a selection. Judging from what I got from him, Cazdelbo must have carried a very fine and unusual stock for his time. I acquired lithographs by Matisse, Derain, and Arthur Davies. I never had these prints framed and in the 1940s I sold them for a pittance to a dentist in Chicago. I am not quite sure why I did this. Certainly I didn't need the

money. My guess is that it indicated my ambivalence about collecting art, a hobby which had been imposed on me by my mother. Perhaps I parted with these works so easily because the choices, in
effect, had never really been mine. With Mother's encouragement
(and my parents' money) I acquired several prints by French artists
during a family trip to Europe in 1925. In addition I acquired a few
works by American printmakers which probably came from exhibitions sponsored by the Des Moines Association of Fine Arts. Most of
these early acquisitions were given to the Des Moines Art Center
soon after its opening in 1948. These include prints by French artists
Marie Laurencin, Louis Legrand, Milly Possoz, and Auguste Brouet,
and by American artists Frank Benson and Joseph Pennell.

There were also visits with Mother to the Art Institute in Chicago
where I was impressed with the Monet haystacks and a full-length
portrait by Cecelia Beaux. On our second trip to Europe in 1925 I
went with Mother to art museums while Father and Joe went in other
directions. Mother was always careful to seek out every work
awarded three stars in *Baedeker*'s guidebook. More interesting to me
than museums were the antique shops in Europe. I acquired this interest from Mother who was especially interested in collecting old
silver. Often, while the family was eating lunch I would go off on my
own in search of interesting mementos. These ranged from a pair of
hand-painted porcelain bottles from Paris and four silver teaspoons
from Tours, to a seventeenth-century brass pocket compass and sun-
dial from Geneva. I don't know what became of the bottles, which
stood on my dresser for many years. I still have the spoons. A few
years ago I offered the sundial/compass to the Adler Planetarium in
Chicago. They pronounced it a valuable piece and were delighted to
accept it for their collection. I also looked for fans for Aunt Ettie's collection and was often successful in my search. In fact, I became so interested in old fans that in 1928 I wrote an article based on Aunt
Ettie's collection that I sold to *Arts and Decoration* magazine (August
1928, 29:44–45) under the name of Louise Allison. It is difficult for
me now to understand what made me feel so unworthy that I needed
to publish under a pseudonym, and it seems strange that Mother did
not protest the decision to conceal my authorship. As I recall, I felt
that because I was writing about my aunt's collection and because
she furnished all the photographs, I really didn't deserve much
credit. In fact, my desire for self-effacement was so strong that I
didn't even bother to save a copy of the magazine in which my article
was published. Years later I found one through a secondhand dealer.

The most famous antique I ever acquired was an antique "lady's"

desk which Flora Dunlap gave me after I was married. She had purchased this desk in Baltimore about 1920 and had it in her home for
many years. I had always admired this desk and was delighted when
Flora said she wanted me to have it. It had delicate inlaid wood, secret drawers, and eglomé panels—black glass with figures painted in
gold. The desk had been pronounced a rare piece, made in Baltimore
about 1800, by the curator of the American wing of the Metropolitan
Museum. In 1961 when Jackie Kennedy started redecorating the
White House with period furniture I decided that this desk would be
more appropriate there than in my home and the curator of the
White House accepted it without question. She arranged for an ap-
praisal which came in at $20,000. The desk was pronounced one of
the rarest prizes in the White House and given a place of honor in
the Green Room. In February 1962, Jackie Kennedy gave a televised
tour of the redecorated White House in the course of which she
spoke glowingly of my desk and said it was the first unsolicited piece
of fine furniture to be received. She wished there were more people
like Mrs. Noun. This was at the height of the Kennedys' popularity
and as a result of Jackie's approbation I was deluged with phone calls
and mail from long-lost relatives and friends as well as numerous
strangers. One woman who collected buttons belonging to famous
people asked me to send a piece for her collection. I satisfied her
with one provided by my friend, Jeanette Eyerly, from her mother's
button box.

In September 1962 I had a call from Maxine Cheshire of the
Washington Post which went something like this: "Are you the lady
who gave the desk to the White House?" I said I was. Then, "Have you
heard that they are saying it is a fake?" No I hadn't. Apparently there
was talk around Washington that the desk might be a 1900 copy of an
older piece and there were plans to quietly remove it from the Green
Room. Obviously, with Cheshire on the trail, there was to be no quiet
removal. I decided that the best thing to do was to ask for the desk
back and the White House was happy to comply. Cheshire's story
about the desk was headed, "White House Finds Green Room Desk is
$20,000 Fake." (*Washington Post*, September 6, 1962) Needless to say,
an agent from the Bureau of Internal Revenue was on my doorstep
the next day. When the rash of stories about the removal of the desk
was over, I gave the desk to the Iowa Children's Home Society with
the stipulation that they sell it at auction. The piece brought $1,500.

3

EDUCATION AND TRAVEL

Mother's first choice of a college for me would have been Vassar or Wellesley where she had registered me almost as soon as I was born, but she felt that the Des Moines schools did not offer sufficient preparation to enable me to pass the College Board examinations necessary for entrance to Ivy League schools. (College Boards were not required when my sister Ruth went to Vassar.) On the other hand, she refused to send me away to a private preparatory school since she was a firm believer in public education. Grinnell seemed a suitable college for me. It was a small school with no sororities or fraternities as social barriers, and my brother, who graduated from Grinnell the year I entered, had been very happy there. At Grinnell I found my classes reasonably satisfactory although I later realized that with few exceptions, the quality of teaching was not too good. My roommate at Grinnell was Ginny Munn, a high school friend. She was an outgoing, friendly person who was popular with both the male and female students. My problem was that the male students paid no attention to me and I found myself weekend after weekend sitting alone while Ginny and other women in the dormitory were out with their dates. When I visited Ginny a few years ago she recalled coming back to the dorm from a date one evening and finding me in tears. This incident was apparently so painful that I had completely suppressed the memory of it. During my sophomore year at Grinnell I decided that the solution to my problem was to transfer to a women's college for my last two years where I would have fewer social pressures. Madge Prouty (now Madge Neufeld), with whom I had gone to school since kindergarten, and I both applied to Barnard College in New York City. I was taken aback when Madge was accepted and I was not. With Madge's permission, I checked her scholastic record and found that over the years my grades were consistently higher than hers. I was Jewish and Madge was not. It seemed obvious that I was a victim of the Jewish quota at Barnard and my mother was furious. When she complained to Barnard the school sent word to apply again the next semester, which I did. I was accepted, but by this time I had lost my taste for Barnard and decided on Wellesley, where my application was of such long standing that I must have been at the top of the list for transfers.

Mother went with me to Wellesley in the fall of 1927 to see that I was properly settled. It never occurred to me to tell her that I didn't need, or even want, her help. She was pleased with my roommate, Luise Meyer, a very worldly-wise young woman from San Francisco, and said she thought this type of person would be good for me. Mother was obviously telling me that I needed more sophistication. Luise was stylish (all her clothes came from I. Magnin in San Francisco), brilliant, popular with men, and very socially ambitious. In fact, we had so little in common that at the end of the first semester she suggested we both move to single rooms. I felt rejected but on the other hand I was glad to be living by myself. I did have a few dates while at Wellesley but between my shyness and my feeling that there must be something wrong with any man who would want to go out with me my social life was limited. I tried to conform to expectations by taking to heart the advice of my cousin Ansel, at Harvard, who advised me that I shouldn't let men know that I had any brains.

My college major was history and my minor was English and with the exception of gym, which I almost flunked, my grades were above average at Wellesley. However, at the end of my first year there, the dean called me to her office and announced that I must go to summer school and take six hours of extra credit. When I asked her why, she said it was because I had come from an inferior school. This made no sense since Wellesley had accepted me without any conditions, and all the dean wanted me to do was to go to any school, no matter what its academic standing, take any courses I wanted to, and earn six hours of credit with at least a C grade. I was very resentful about this but never thought to fight this unfair requirement. My response was to enroll at Drake University for a three-week summer session and take three easy courses for which I refused to do more than minimal studying. Just before Christmas vacation my senior year at Wellesley, Mother sent Flora Dunlap to tell me that my father had been diagnosed as having incurable cancer and that Mother thought I should drop out of school immediately. This meant that I couldn't even finish the semester at Wellesley. I didn't question Mother's judgment at the time and, never having had to face the impending death of anyone in my family, I thought if Mother wanted me at home, it must be the proper thing to do. In retrospect, however, it is hard to understand why she wanted me there when my brother and sister were both still living at home. In addition, she had all the household help she needed. I knew that if I quit school in the middle of my senior year, however, I might never go back again, so I suggested that I return to Grinnell where I could be home on weekends. Mother agreed to this plan. I got a special dispensation from Grinnell that permitted me to return for the last half of my senior year, and thanks to the extra summer school credits I had earned, I had very little work to make up. ✓

There was one condition on my return to Grinnell imposed by the dean of women. She feared I might have learned to smoke while in the East and she made me promise that I wouldn't use cigarettes when I came back. As a matter of fact I had learned to smoke my first year at Grinnell hiding behind the grade school across the street from the women's dorms. (Men, in contrast to women, were permitted to smoke at Grinnell.) I might never have started smoking if my father had offered me the same substantial bribe which he had offered my bother, Joe, for not smoking until he was twenty-five. All Ruth and I were offered was our parents' disapproval. I soon found that in my year and a half away, smoking had become a common occurrence in the women's dorms at Grinnell. Although I kept my promise I became more irked as the semester progressed. I decided to bring up the issue of smoking at a meeting of the women's student government at the end of the year but almost lost my nerve when I saw the dean in the audience. However, I did manage to say a few words concerning the need for a change in rules. This was my first public protest and I shall never forget the fear and trembling with which it was made. In the present antitobacco atmosphere, the smoking issue seems strange; but when I was in school smoking was a symbol of emancipation for women. Now it is looked on as a symbol of death. I kept on smoking until I was past forty and then I resolved to give it up because I was so addicted. This was one of the hardest things I ever did.

Father died in April 1929 and I graduated from college a few weeks later with no idea of what I would do next. I found that Mother, unbeknownst to me, had investigated graduate courses in art history and decided that Radcliffe/Harvard was the place for me to go. (Although all graduate work was at Harvard, women were required to register as Radcliffe students.) It especially appealed to her because of Paul Sachs's museum course. Having no goal in life other than eventual marriage, I readily agreed to her suggestion that I take off for Harvard in the fall. This meant a reprieve from living at home. Apparently Harvard accepted anyone with a good academic record and enough money to pay tuition because I certainly had no background for graduate work in art other than an art survey course at Wellesley during my senior year, which was not completed because of my leaving school at Christmas time.

At Harvard I had no problem with art history courses where no background was expected, but Professor Sachs's museum course was another matter. Classes met in the living room of his home, "Shady Hill," which was full of art objects used for teaching purposes. During our first class he held up a painting and asked for identification. It turned out to be a Flemish painting with some major defect. My ignorance was so abysmal that I had never even heard of the Flemish school of art! After that I tried to hide behind some large piece of furniture so I wouldn't be noticed. Eventually, when I had learned art lingo and had acquired some art history background, I became less fearful of this dynamic, cocky little man. I found the study of art history a satisfying experience in contrast to the frustrations of trying to produce studio art. Here I could use my mind instead of struggling to be creative with my hands. I returned to Harvard the next year, spending the bulk of my time in the print room of the Fogg Museum where I did independent study, nominally under Professor Sachs but actually under the watchful eye of Laura Dudley, the acting head of the print department. By the end of the 1930–1931 school year I had earned enough credits for a master of arts degree but I was not eligible to receive it until I had fulfilled Harvard's foreign language requirement, which called for a reading knowledge of either French or German and an elementary knowledge of the other. I was able to demonstrate a reading knowledge of French but I had no knowledge of German. I attended a Radcliffe German class for a while but dropped the course because I didn't like the professor. I eventually went to Germany where I learned enough of the language to be able to meet the Harvard language requirement. I was awarded my degree in absentia in the spring of 1933.

During the five years between school and my marriage in 1936, I was like a ship without a rudder—constantly drifting but with no guided direction. When I came home after graduate school, my sister,

Ruth, was married and had a home of her own. My brother, Joe, was practicing law and living at home. In those days unmarried sons and daughters were expected to live with their parents until they either got married or moved to another city. Mother was now a widow and free to travel and she assumed that I would want to travel with her. As far as I was concerned, I could see no choice as long as Mother wanted me to go with her. Open rebellion was unthinkable for a person of my disposition but I did at times find other ways of scotching Mother's travel plans, especially when it came to automobile trips. I can recall the time I drove her to visit relatives in Milwaukee when I was so tense and unhappy about the driving that I developed pain in my neck and shoulders. I would drive a couple of hours and say I was exhausted and needed a rest. It took a long time for us to make that trip and Mother never asked me to take her on another automobile journey. I went to Jasper Park in the Canadian Rockies with her one summer and at another time to Lake Bemidji in Minnesota. In addition, we were together during three trips to Europe.

We left for the first of these trips in the fall of 1931 with Aileen Cohen (now Aileen Frank), my Des Moines friend who had also studied at the Fogg the previous year. I didn't return until the summer of 1932. This was the first European trip in which I was truly a museum enthusiast. This time Aileen and I led the way to museums and Mother followed. We started our trip in Paris and then went on to Germany, arriving in Italy in early fall to spend the winter. I think we saw every important (and some not so important) Renaissance work of art from Milan to Naples. From Naples we took a boat to Sicily, landing in Palermo where Aileen sailed for home.

I was not happy about being left alone with Mother. What I really wanted to do was to go to Germany on my own to learn the language there. Instead of confronting Mother directly with a request to leave me, I just decided to wait it out until she got tired of traveling and went home. A good deal of the time I just sulked. Mother resented my going to my room right after dinner each night and at times insisted on my spending the evening sitting in hotel parlors with her. I can recall one evening when I looked so dejected that a stranger came over and asked if I were not feeling well. Mother took great satisfaction in my embarrassment. Our Sicilian tour ended at Taormina, a delightful resort village overlooking the Ionian Sea. Here I had a respite from Mother's constant company in a pension where we met congenial people. During this stay Mother arranged for a young Dutch artist, G. V. A. Roling, who had won a fellowship to work in Italy, to make a pastel portrait of me. He had a studio near the coast and I would walk down from the town for my sittings through groves of blooming almond trees. It was a beautiful time of the year to be in Sicily. The portrait, which I still have, has stood the test of time as a competent, even sensitive work. Whether or not it was a good likeness of me at the time is hard for me to tell. After several weeks in Taormina Mother still showed no signs of wanting to go home, so we decided to go back to Florence, which we had visited earlier in the trip. Here I ran into Margaret Wuerpel, a friend from graduate school, who was staying at a pension near our hotel. I escaped Mother's constant company by moving in with Margaret. By this time I think Mother was really anxious to go home but she still didn't want to leave me alone in Europe although she never said so expressly.

Mother knew I wanted to study in Germany but hesitated about having me go there because of the political situation. In the presidential elections in March Hitler had received enough votes to force a runoff election with the current president, General Paul von Hindenburg, and Mother was concerned that Hitler might come to power. However, when Hindenburg won the runoff election in April, Mother finally agreed to let me go on my own, but not before accompanying me to Berlin and seeing me safely ensconced in a pension where I had some acquaintances, Elizabeth and Walter Moak. Walter headed the Berlin office of an American bank. We were the only Americans staying at the pension, and I would have a cocktail before dinner with them every day before going downstairs to the dining room. All the other residents of the pension were Germans but they didn't speak English and I never got to know them on a social basis. The proprietor of the pension was a "Frau Professor" who gave us free ice for our cocktails and always reminded us of this when we asked for any other favor. I arranged for German lessons with a teacher who was willing to come to the pension several times a week. At first she gave me children's literature to translate because it was easy, but after a few weeks of this I told her I would like something more interesting. So she set me to work on a bloody story about two escaped prisoners who hid in a haystack while men with pitchforks probed the stack for their presence. I can't remember if these men ever escaped alive. Perhaps I abandoned the story midstream. In addition to my German lessons, my days in Berlin were mainly occupied by almost daily visits to the Kaiser Friederich Museum where I inspected box after box of old master prints and drawings. My education at Harvard had not prepared me to look at any work of art not validated by historians so I was completely uninterested in finding out what was going on in the contemporary Berlin art scene.

Basically, I am not a linguist. Not only are foreign languages difficult for me to learn, but I am very hesitant about trying to speak
them. One day I called on a German couple whom friends suggested I
contact. They were appalled at my very limited knowledge of German and suggested that I needed to live with a German family where
I would be forced to use the language. Furthermore, they knew just
the family who would help me. So although I was very happy at the
pension where I was staying, I decided to try living with this family. I
soon found myself in a situation which distressed me very much.
The husband was unemployed and it soon became evident that the
family was very hard up. My bedroom in their apartment had belonged to the son who was moved into the dining room to make room
for me. But what made me most uncomfortable was being served
meat and other delicacies while the parents and their two children
were eating boiled potatoes. I ate as many meals out as possible but
still found the situation very depressing. After a couple of weeks, I
decided to move back to the pension. I told the family that my friend,
Margaret Wuerpel, was ill and coming to Berlin so I could look after
her. They insisted that she stay with them. They would give her the
other child's bedroom. I insisted that this would inconvenience them
too much. So I set a date for my departure and made a point of having
lunch with the family on the day I left. I felt a very chilly atmosphere
around the table. I can remember trying to make conversation in my
limited German. "In Sicily they eat goat meat," I recall saying. The
answer to this and any other attempt at pleasantry was a cool "Ja."
While I was packing to leave after lunch the wife came in and told me
her husband said they were not running a hotel and that I owed them
an extra month's rent. So I paid up and went on my way with a guilty
feeling about abandoning this family in need, but delighted to be
back at the pension again.

There was a good deal of talk about the Nazis when I was in
Berlin and I knew that some people at the pension were sympathetic
to their cause, which in today's terms would be somewhat comparable to sympathy with the John Birch Society—deplorable but not
horrifying. I thought it would be interesting to hear Hitler address a
mass meeting but I never got around to it. There was an election
while I was in Berlin and it seemed advisable to stay home that day.
Walter Moak told us that evening about sending his home office a ca-
blegram stating that all was quiet during this election. While he was
still in the cable office a shot came through the window. Still, none of
us realized the seriousness of the situation. I never dreamed that
Hitler might come to power until I got to England that summer and

started reading the English newspapers about the situation in Germany. I became concerned about my wardrobe trunk, which I had left in Berlin in care of the Hamburg-American steamship line. Yet, uncertain as the situation seemed to be, who except Hitler himself would dream that in the twentieth century the greatest mass pogrom in history was about to take place? Even Dorothy Thompson, the well-known American journalist who interviewed Hitler about this time, decided "in less than 50 seconds" that he was a man of "startling insignificance" who would never be dictator of Germany.*

While I was in Berlin I enjoyed going to symphony concerts under the direction of Wilhelm Furtwängler, but what impressed me most in the city were the large numbers of gays and lesbians I saw everywhere. They were easily identified because the men wore gold bracelets and the women mannish suits. One evening I went with the Moaks to a nightclub where the entertainers were men in drag. All this was a new experience for me. I had first learned that there was such a thing as homosexuality at Grinnell where it was whispered that two women whom I liked very much did strange things in bed. At that time I didn't even know that there was a word for such behavior. The open avowal of homosexuality along with the presence of large numbers of prositutes on the streets of Berlin gave me the impression of its being a licentious city. I found this behavior more interesting than shocking.

When I left Berlin in the summer of 1932, I met Margaret Wuerpel in Brussels. After visiting museums in Belgium and Holland we went on to London where I spent a good deal of time in the print room of the British Museum. From London we set out on a tour of England, going by local bus from place to place. We stopped in Salisbury to see the cathedral and I still have an antique brass candlestick which I purchased there. From southern England we went to Cornwall and then to Wales where I was amazed to find that many people spoke Welsh rather than English. The trip seemed very strenuous to me but I attributed this feeling to the difficulties of meeting local bus schedules rather than to my own physical condition. When I found myself in a hotel bar at ten in the morning ordering a shot of scotch to help keep me going, I should have realized there was something wrong. However, I continued on to Liverpool where I came down with a bad head cold and went to bed. I remember vividly spending a whole day crying, not because of any specific incident, just because I felt so weak and helpless. Margaret, who planned to sail home from Scotland in a few days was distressed and wanted to

*As quoted in the New York Times Book Review, February 5, 1989, p. 5.

take me back to London. I insisted I could get there on my own. I arranged for a room at the English Speaking Union and for the Union to make a doctor's appointment for me. The doctor took one look at me and said I was severely anemic. He never bothered to take a blood test. (My Des Moines doctor, astonished by this lack of scientific evidence, later confirmed the diagnosis.) I had hoped to go to Spain from England despite the fact that there was some shooting going on there but when I got sick I reluctantly decided to sail for home.

I spent the winter of 1932–1933 at home recuperating, and the following spring Harvard sent its German language examination to Drake University so I could take it in Des Moines. I passed the exam and was eligible for my master's degree. Now I was ready to start out in a career in the art world. My ambition was to work in a museum print room but when I went back to Harvard to ask Professor Sachs for help in finding a job, he just shook his head and commented, "Why don't you just go home and get married." He said it would be impossible to place me even as a volunteer. I was so humiliated by Sachs's attitude that it took years—in fact until the arrival of the current feminist movement—before I could even talk about it. At the time this rejection seemed a denigration of my personal worth. I now realize that it was a reflection of his attitude toward women; in other words, a prime example of sexism.

Despite Sachs's discouragement I went to New York in the fall to look for work in the art field. Both my expectations and my self-esteem were so low that I would have been satisfied with the most menial job, which is what I ended up with. The process of job hunting was one of the most trying experiences of my life. I was so painfully insecure and shy that it took the utmost willpower to gather enough courage to apply for a position. I have no memory of how many places I went, but I suspect they were few. I do recall visiting with a woman at the College Art Association about the possibility of a job and her astonishment that I waited until near the end of my interview to tell her I had a Master of Arts degree. My abject modesty was indeed self-destructive. I finally landed a temporary job doing clerical work at an exhibition titled "A Mile of American Art" in Rockefeller Center. This building had just been completed and the exhibition filled much of the unrented space in the lower level. It comprised a broad survey of current work and was, in fact, my first exposure to contemporary American art. My first assignment was addressing envelopes. Later I may have done a little docent work but I am not sure. When the Rockefeller Center show closed I could see no prospect of other work, so I decided to head for home and return to New York in the fall to look for another job.

Mother's home was a haven when I couldn't find more satisfying things to do but I took every opportunity to get away as much as possible. In the summer of 1934 I went to Europe once again. My traveling companion was a Des Moines friend, Betty Brine (later Betty Blakemore). We traveled second class on the ship going over—the first of my European trips when I hadn't gone first class. Our roommate was a working-class young woman who must have thought us extremely snobbish. We stayed up most of the night and slept most of the day and she did the opposite. We had no interest in her and we hardly spoke to her the whole trip. The first part of our trip was spent in Normandy and Brittany. We went to Bayeux to see the famous tapestries (really embroideries) but I have a less distinct memory of them than I do of the charming inn where we stayed and the delicious food served in an attractive courtyard. In Brittany we went to a festival where we saw people in traditional dress. First Betty and then I came down with hives from eating too much shellfish. The highlight of our Paris stay was donning our evening dresses and going to a very elegant small nightclub with Fred Maytag, scion of the Maytag washing machine family. We drank champagne and listened to a Hungarian orchestra play popular tunes such as Cole Porter's "Smoke Gets in Your Eyes" until the wee hours of the morning. We assumed that this kind of an outing was not unusual for Fred, but his wife, Ellen, whom he married shortly after his return, tells me that he never forgot that evening with us in Paris.

From Paris we went to London where we met Mother for a trip through the English countryside. Mother had spent the early part of the summer traveling in Scandinavia with her friend, Flora Dunlap. She doubtless must have suggested joining us in England because I never would have invited her. She rented a car with a driver called "Pike" to take us on this tour. I assume Pike was his last name. He was very correct in demeanor and maintained a poker face at all times. Betty and I did our best to make him smile but Mother thought we were getting too familiar.

When I returned home from Europe in the late summer of 1934, I took a short course in speed-writing (most educated women of my generation ended up as secretaries) and returned to New York to look for another job. This time I found a position as secretary to Arthur Pope, one of my Harvard professors, who was on leave of absence for the year to work for the Carnegie Foundation for the Advancement of Teaching. My work was far from arduous. It consisted of taking dictation for a very limited number of letters and of typing copy for a book that Pope was writing. Fortunately, Professor Pope had the utmost tolerance for my lack of skill and never complained about the quality of my work. My friend, Frances Clark (now Frances Braxton), a Vassar graduate who was secretary for an RCA executive with offices nearby, would come to my aid when needed by meeting me for lunch and helping me transcribe my speed-writing notes. Pope returned to Boston in the late spring of 1935, and I once again returned to Des Moines with no sense of direction to my life.

Mother complained that with all my education I was doing nothing to share it with others. She organized a group of women who came to our house where I gave a series of talks on the history of prints. I had a deep sense of unease that educating a group of society women wasn't what I really wanted to do but I didn't see any alternative. Mother also arranged for me to give a talk on prints at Younkers' tea room, which I docilely agreed to do, although speaking in public was painfully embarrassing for me. Furthermore, my lack of self-assurance gave me the feeling that I was a failure at this sort of thing.

Over the Christmas holidays in 1935–1936 I went to Guatemala with a group organized by Hubert Herring, who had come to Des Moines to lecture in the first adult education program in the city. This was an interesting group, among them René d'Harnoncourt, later director of the Museum of Modern Art in New York; Erna Fergusson, a travel writer; and a young woman archeologist from the University of Pennsylvania. We went on a United Fruit boat from New York and watched the loading of bananas after we landed in Guatemala. Our train made a special stop on the way up to Guatemala City so we could see important Mayan stelae standing in the nearby jungle. I found the Guatemala Indian population fascinating, especially the colorful, handwoven dress of the women—each village with its own distinctive costume. I came home with a number of beautiful pieces of weaving—mostly items of native dress—as the industry for making clothing for tourists was still undeveloped. In some villages we were greeted with marimba music, and at Chichicastenango we visited with the priest of the imposing church where Indians were performing ancient religious rites on the entrance porch. In Guatemala City I met an anthropologist from the University of Chicago who told me, much to my surprise, that he found the Indians in Tama, Iowa, more interesting than those in Guatemala.

In the summer of 1936 I again went to Europe with Mother. Our ship going over was crowded with athletes and others, including the actress Helen Hayes and her husband, Charles MacArthur, who were headed for the Olympic games in Berlin. By this time Hitler was in power and we had no desire to go to Germany. We disembarked in Ireland where a driver with a winning personality, named Kyle, met us and took us on a tour of the country. The last part of our trip was in Norway, Sweden, and Denmark. In Scandinavia I was fascinated with the contemporary architecture and the modern designs in household utensils and furniture. I came home with some handwoven place mats, stainless steel baking dishes, and handcrafted pieces of Swedish silver to use, as Mother would say, "When you have a home of your own."

Louise Rosenfield

Rose Frankel, Oskaloosa, Iowa, 1896.

Meyer Rosenfield

Louise, Joe, and Ruth Rosenfield

Greenwood School's 1921 graduating class.

Joe Rosenfield, Meyer Rosenfield, Aunt Ettie
Pfeifer, Rose Rosenfield, and Louise
Rosenfield, taken on the steps of Babette
Frankel's terrace, around 1923.

Childhood home of Louise Rosenfield Noun,
207 Thirty-seventh Street, Des Moines, Iowa.
(David Penney photo, 1989)

*A corner of Rose Rosenfield's garden at 207
Thirty-seventh Street, 1953. (The Iowan photo)*

Babette Frankel, 1925.

Rose Rosenfield aboard ship en route to Scandinavia, 1934. (Des Moines Register photo)

Louise Rosenfield, about 1934.

Rose Rosenfield in her garden, 1953. (The *Iowan* photo)

Major and Mrs. M. H. Noun, with boxer dog,
Duchess, at their home at 3511 St. Johns
Road, October 1945.

Antique desk given to the White House. (Des
Moines Register photo)

4

ART CENTER VOLUNTEER

By 1936 I had abandoned my dream of being a museum professional and had convinced myself that as a volunteer I could put to good use my training in art history and museum management. This was a mistake in judgment because I soon found many roadblocks in the way of my making any substantial contribution to the development or management of the Art Center. In fact my art-connected activities over the years have proved to be as frustrating as they have been fulfilling.

In 1938 I was elected to the board of the Des Moines Association of Fine Arts, a group which was trying to keep art interest in the city alive until funds from the estate of James D. Edmundson could be used to build and maintain a museum. Edmundson had died in 1933, leaving a substantial bequest for museum purposes, but his will stated that funds for the museum could not be made available for at least ten years after his death. The Fine Arts Association had traditionally used an art gallery in the public library for exhibition purposes, but at the time I joined the board a decision was made to establish its own gallery. The second floor of an old two-story building between Sixth and Seventh on Walnut Street was rented and remodeled into galleries and studio space. The Art Association gallery was formally opened in November 1938 and continued to operate until 1944 when funds from the Edmundson estate were available for building and operating a museum. At this time the Fine Arts Association considered its mission as an interim organization complete, so it turned over its gallery space and its assets, including works of art, to the Edmundson Art Foundation and went out of business.

I enjoyed working with the Fine Arts Association. We were a group of enthusiastic and energetic people—men and women working together for a common cause. I found a different atmosphere, however, in my contacts with leaders of the Edmundson Art Foundation. This group was headed by the cartoonist Jay N. Darling, with whom Mother had served on the Park Board. He was a male chauvinist of the first order. Darling, along with other Edmundson trustees, felt that women were not capable of handling money and therefore should not be allowed to sit on their board. Instead, Darling set up subsidiary groups where women could do the work while the male trustees handled the funds and maintained ultimate control.

My first contact with Darling was in 1940 when I accepted an invitation from him to be a member of a committee headed by Forest Huttenlocher to advise the trustees on questions concerning design of the proposed museum building and to make recommendations concerning its use. Here, I thought, was my great opportunity to have real input into planning the new museum. I proved to be greatly mistaken. Instead of wanting advice, all Darling wanted was a committee to establish good relations with other community groups by listening to their ideas of what a museum should be. From time to time we were shown sketches of buildings proposed by architects whom the trustees were considering using, but we never had any say as to who these architects should be. When we were asked to approve a proposed design that looked like a Greek temple, I decided to resign from the committee. I did not want to be associated in any way with such an obsolete and unsuitable style of architecture, and after four years on the committee, I was fed up with being used for public relations purposes only.

In January 1944, I sent Darling a letter of resignation to Captiva, Florida, where he had a winter home. I told him that I no longer wanted to continue my membership on a committee that implied responsibility for decisions in which I had no part. Darling was greatly irritated by my resignation. He accused me of deserting the ship and called my resignation an "insurrection." If my decision was final, he said, he would "just have to make the best of it." Not too long after my resignation from the advisory committee I was both surprised and pleased to learn that the Edmundson trustees were considering hiring Eliel Saarinen, the noted Finnish architect, to design the Des Moines Art Center.

It seemed to me at that time that my troubles with Darling were largely due to my being a woman and therefore unwelcome in any truly responsible position in planning the new museum. It never occurred to me that I was also unwelcome because I am a Jew. This fact was revealed to me a few years ago when a 1942 letter from Darling to Gardner Cowles, Sr., was called to my attention. In this letter (written two years before I resigned from the advisory committee) Darling bemoaned the lack of interest in the proposed museum and the difficulty of finding good members for the advisory committee. He then went on to complain that the "Rosenfield branch of the Jewish crowd" (meaning me) was too eager to help and was edging in toward the center of control. He even accused me of frequently suggesting other Jews for committee membership. "What is even more startling," he said, is that "the representatives of that race display more energy and interest than the rest of our cooperators." Darling said he certainly welcomed the efforts of Jews, but he didn't want the museum project to become top-heavy with them. Ironically, in correspondence with me a few months before his death twenty years later Darling congratulated me on my article in the Des Moines Register deploring the exclusion of Jews from Wakonda Club. He added that so far as he knew, "the racial distinction has never even been thought of in the activities of the Des Moines Art Center." "It is too bad," he said, "you weren't born twenty years sooner so that J. D. Edmundson could have put you on the original board of trustees. What we needed more than anything else was somebody who knew something about the arts." Darling certainly had a short memory. It is difficult to deal with the kind of anti-Semitism that praises one to one's face while stabbing one in the back.

Shortly after the Fine Arts Association dissolved in 1944, the Edmundson trustees, at Darling's suggestion, decided to appoint a subsidiary board to work with Paul Parker, whom the trustees had hired as director. This board would be responsible for fund-raising and for day-to-day operation of the proposed museum, which was to be called the Des Moines Art Center. The trustees, however, reserved the right to hire and fire the director, decide on acquisitions, and maintain financial control. This was obviously an attempt to maintain control of the institution while having others do all the work. This new board was known as the Des Moines Art Center Association. Members were largely drawn from persons who had been active in the former Association of Fine Arts. I joined this board realizing that the set-up was far from ideal but it was the only choice I had if I wanted to have a part in organizing the new museum. Under Parker's direction, we developed plans for activities and interviewed staff. Most important, we launched a membership drive which brought in 2,200 members. The Edmundson trustees were delighted to have their work done for them, but the honeymoon was short. Soon after the Art Center opened in the spring of 1949, Paul Parker resigned because the trustees reserved for themselves the right to make purchases of works of art and to accept gifts without the director's prior approval. Our operating board had to stand by helplessly in this conflict between the director and the Art Center trustees. We liked Parker but had no power to influence trustee policies. Because of our frustration over our powerless position we asked the trustees to amalgamate our board with theirs so that there would be a single entity controlling museum policy. The trustees refused to consider our request. For one thing, it would have meant making women trustees and this was completely unacceptable. In addition, it would have meant accepting people like me who were not in sympathy with the conservative taste in art of most of the trustees. The trustees would have liked the operating board to stay in business because we were useful and offered various concessions which would still have left us completely subservient to them. They remained adamant, however, in their refusal to consider a single board. The operating board finally decided that the only way to achieve unified control was for all members of our board to resign. We did this in mid-November 1949, thus forcing the trustees to assume full responsibility for the operation of the Center. With no subsidiary group of volunteers to do the nitty-gritty work of running the Art Center membership drive, the trustees soon found it expedient to add women to their board to undertake this time-consuming job.

My resignation from the operating board left me once more on the outside as far as Art Center operations were concerned. I was angry with the trustees for their stiff-necked attitudes and frustrated because I wanted so much to be a part of this venture. The situation changed in 1956 when Mother gave the Art Center $25,000 to be spent for the purchase of contemporary art. Mother had great respect for Dwight Kirsch, director of the Art Center from 1950 to 1958, and she wanted to honor him with this gift. I feel confident that she was not trying to buy me a place on the board. She was too proud to have ever done a thing like that. Anyway, a few months after Mother's gift was received I was invited to join the board of trustees. When my Uncle Henry, who had been named a trustee in Edmundson's will, informed me of my election, he was apologetic about the timing of this invitation but he hoped I would accept it nonetheless. I did, but not without a sense of humiliation and resentment of the fact that my position was, in effect, purchased by Mother. Women had been serving on the board for seven years. If the board had wanted me for my knowledge and not because of my mother's money they could have asked me sooner. Although I did not take note of the fact at the time, I now realize that I was the first Jew, except for the three named by Edmundson in his will, ever to become an Art Center trustee.

As soon as I joined the Art Center board I paid my dues, so to speak, by heading a very successful membership drive. Dwight Kirsch was a person whom I liked personally and whom I respected for his knowledge of art. He was an excellent teacher and I enjoyed serving on the acquisition committee under his direction. A couple of years after Dwight's departure, I was pleased when David Kruidenier, president of the Art Center board, asked me to chair the acquisition committee. I looked forward to working with the director, Tom Tibbs, who had recently come to the Art Center from New York where he headed the Museum of Contemporary Crafts. Unfortunately, this was not a pleasant experience. One of the first pictures Tibbs presented for purchase consideration was purportedly by Jacob van Ruisdael, a seventeenth-century Dutch landscape painter. In spite of the fact that this picture represented a deviation from the Art Center's policy of acquiring nineteenth- and twentieth-century art, the acquisition committee, hesitating to turn down the director's first recommendation, gave reluctant approval to the purchase. The trustees, acting on the committee recommendation, also gave their approval. Soon after the trustees' meeting and before the picture was paid for, I heard rumors that the Ruisdael came from an unreliable dealer. I called David Kruidenier and explained the problem to him and suggested that we withhold payment until we learned more about the painting. I heard nothing from David, but a week after my call, Tibbs phoned me. "I understand that you have questions about the Ruisdael painting," he said. I replied that I did. "Well, that is too bad," he responded, "the picture is already paid for." David had evidently told him to go ahead and pay for the picture despite my questions. (Several months later he apologized.) I was very bitter that my suggestion had been ignored and I showed no restraint in expressing my anger to Tibbs. (I now realize it would have been more appropriate to tell David how I felt about the matter.) In any event, my own subsequent investigation convinced me that the picture was a fake, a judgment that was upheld nine years later by authorities who were asked to examine the Ruisdael. The Art Center subsequently sued the dealer to recover the $24,000 paid for the painting but the suit was dismissed on the grounds that the six-year statute of limitations had run out. This painting was subsequently deaccessioned and sold for $3,500. In 1963 when my second three-year term was up as an Art Center trustee, I decided to get off the board. The Art Center at this time did not have a rotating board but I felt that six years was long enough for anyone to serve. In addition, I didn't enjoy working with a director for whom I had no respect.

My happiest relationship with the Art Center was from 1969 to 1984, during Jim Demetrion's term as director. I have the deepest respect for Jim's knowledge of art and for his great personal integrity. He was also perceptive enough to recognize that I could be useful to the Art Center in a professional way. He hired me part-time in 1970 to help catalog the Art Center's collection. Later, I wrote an essay on the Iowa-born sculptor, Abastenia St. Leger Eberle, for the catalog of an exhibition of her work which I helped organize. I also wrote a history of the Des Moines Art Center for the catalog of its permanent collection. Jim has also been most helpful in my efforts to build my personal collection of art by women. During the time Jim was director, I was invited to become an honorary trustee of the Art Center but I declined. My relationship with the Art Center at this point was better than it had ever been and I did not care to be the recipient of an empty honor. "My decision stems from a desire to limit my activities to those in which I feel I can make some meaningful contribution," I said in my response. "While the position of honorary trustee would add luster to my obituary, I can see no way in which it would offer new avenues of meaningful association with the Art Center. My decision does not indicate any lack of interest in, or lack of support of, the Art Center," I continued. "It simply means that with age has come some knowledge of how I want to order my priorities." What I did not say was that I still resented the slights I suffered during the early days of the Art Center and that an honorary membership at this late date could not compensate for these slights even though the current trustees were blameless.

5

MARRIAGE AND MOTHERHOOD

By the mid-1930s I realized that I would be at home unless I decided to get married. I had my first serious love affair during my second winter in New York, but the man I was interested in had no intention of marrying me. I met Maurie Noun sometime in 1933 or 1934 at a party at the Hyperion country club. After that we saw a good deal of each other. Maurie was a dermatologist, four years older than I, who had started practicing in Des Moines after interning here.

Maurie was born in Russia but came to this country as a small child. His father was a carpenter and builder and his mother a typical "Jewish mother" whose life was devoted to caring for, and especially cooking for, her six children. Maurie grew up in Minneapolis, worked his way through the University of Minnesota, and went on to study medicine at St. Louis University School of Medicine. He took his dermatological training in New York. When I met him he had a successful practice and was well respected in the community. He was eager to get married. I was hesitant about marrying Maurie because he did not have any of my intellectual interests but I finally decided that he was a decent, hard-working person, not a penniless fortune hunter like my sister's husband, and that I could adjust my life to the role of doctor's wife. I would devote myself to promoting his welfare and also to rearing any children that might result from our marriage. At this time I wasn't sure who I really was or what I wanted out of life so the easiest solution seemed to be to merge my identity with someone else. On Thanksgiving day, 1936, Maurie and I announced our engagement at a family dinner at Mother's house and were married in Mother's living room about three weeks later.

After returning from a wedding trip to Mexico over the Christmas holidays, Maurie and I sublet a furnished apartment for a few months and then rented a furnished house while we looked for a lot on which to build that "home of my own." After a good deal of looking in other sections of Des Moines, we purchased a large lot on St. John's Road bordering the back lot line of Mother's property and adjacent to her tennis court. The selection of this property indicates that although I was eager to get away from Mother, I was far from ready for a complete break. My reasoning at the time was that it would be nice to be near the tennis court (where I hardly ever played). In fact, I wasn't ready to move from the neighborhood where I had grown up. The tennis court was still used by people in the neighborhood and offered a certain amount of social life for us. Although I would not have admitted it at the time, it felt very comfortable to be near Mother and her household retinue. Other neighborhoods seemed like foreign territory to me. During the first two years of my marriage I was occupied largely with planning, building, and furnishing our home, a Williamsburg-style Georgian house, designed by a talented but temperamental architect, Micky McBroom. Since I was paying for the house, Maurie was content to have me do the planning. His main role was to serve as peacemaker when I got into arguments with the architect.

In the 1930s it was taken for granted that a husband should support his wife. No matter what she contributed financially to the marriage, the fiction that the husband always supported his wife must never be challenged. Furthermore, the wife of a professional man must never work for pay. That would demean her husband. In general, the wife was expected to submerge her needs, both intellectual and emotional, to those of her husband. She could help his business by entertaining the right people and enhance his social status by participating in socially correct cultural and charitable enterprises such as the Junior League, the United Way, and music and art associations. She could join a bridge club, a book club, a music club, or take flower-arranging lessons. She was not expected to take an active role in partisan politics or in left-wing causes which might upset the status quo. Every married couple was expected to have children (preferably a boy and a girl) and women were not encouraged to question whether or not they were ready for motherhood. Most wives of professional people had live-in maids. Thursday was maid's day out and if the maid was lucky she got Sunday afternoon and evening off too. Ione, the first maid we had when we moved into our house on St. John's Road, was an attractive and capable divorcée who was a registered nurse. No hospital would hire her because she had been married. Consequently she had to leave her two young children with her parents in Council Bluffs while she earned her living as a household worker in Des Moines. Even with my undeveloped feminist consciousness, Ione's situation seemed outrageous to me.

We moved into our new home in the spring of 1938 but in the fall we left for several months because Maurie decided to return to New York for further dermatological training. That winter in New York was not a happy one for me. We lived in an apartment hotel so I had few household responsibilities. I was eager to improve my cooking skills but the first time I prepared dinner and served it on the drop-leaf table in our living room, the table leaf collapsed and the food all went in Maurie's lap. He decided that there would be no more dinners at home. I am not quite sure why he made this decision but I suspect it was due largely to his many food phobias. He just didn't trust my cooking. At least I got some practice preparing his oatmeal for breakfast every day. At this time I was trying to be the perfect subservient wife so I didn't complain that I needed to be kept busy. I was determined to do only the things Maurie was interested in, and since his interest was mainly medicine, I sat around the apartment a good deal of the time listening to Maurie talk about medicine with his fellow students and learned a lot about the treatment of lupus erythematosus and other dermatological phenomena.

We returned to Des Moines in the spring of 1939 and I settled down to the role of doctor's wife and society matron, which meant that I joined the women's auxiliary to the medical society, went with my husband to medical conventions, entertained other doctors and their spouses at small dinner parties, and became a volunteer worker in the community. I had joined the Des Moines Junior League several years earlier and my volunteer work at this time centered around activities sponsored by the League. These were service-oriented kinds of activities such as driving children to clinics, reading to children at the Junior League Convalescent Home, addressing invitations to the League's annual charity ball, and working at Junior League rummage and book sales. I also helped paint a playhouse at the Junior League Convalescent Home. We used so much paint I am sure it would have been cheaper to hire the work done professionally. I had plenty of time for these activities since we had adequate household help and no children.

During World War II, Maurie enlisted in the army and was sent to Fitzsimmons General Hospital in Denver. I went with him to assume the role of army wife. This meant renting our house in Des Moines and making a home for Maurie wherever he was sent. However, after a few weeks in a miserable motel in Denver, Maurie was ordered overseas. Since our house was rented I reluctantly went back to Mother's home where once again I felt trapped. Fortunately our tenants were soon transferred out of town and I could live in my own home again. Maurie was away for almost three years. His absence, in effect, took away my role as doctor's wife and left me in the role of war widow. In the evening I played bridge with other war widows, and to occupy myself during the day I worked mornings as a volunteer at the women's division of the Polk County war bond office. The director of the women's division was Louise Newcomb, whose mother was a girlhood friend of my mother's in Oskaloosa. Louise put me to work on some unchallenging clerical jobs. I didn't have enough courage to ask for something better, yet I was resentful when other volunteers were given more responsible positions. The final blow came when I went to the Embassy Club for lunch one day with Dannie Rosenfield, my sister-in-law, and found the entire staff of the war bond office with the exception of myself being entertained there by Vernon Clark, director of the project. When I went to work the next day, Louise apologized and said my omission was Vern's fault. I was crushed but unable to express my hurt and anger. I quit shortly after that. Several years later Vern stopped me in a restaurant and said he owed me a long-overdue apology. He blamed Louise for leaving me out. After all these years there is not much use in my assessing blame though I tend to think it was Louise who was at fault. She was known to have a mean streak. What she had against me, I can't imagine.

When Maurie returned from army service in 1945 we adopted a baby girl whom we named Susan. I was pleased when she later decided to add Louise as a middle name. I had never been around small children before and was terrified at the thought of looking after a ten-day-old infant. Before long I found that she wouldn't break when I handled her. I also learned that even tiny babies were human beings and that there was lots I needed to know about rearing a child. We both survived this learning process and Susan has long since forgiven me my shortcomings as a mother. Susan has been able to have a much warmer and more loving relationship with her only child, Jason Flora, than I was able to have with her. For a while, when Susan was a baby, I tried staying at home almost full-time to fulfill my new role as a mother, but I soon found this role too confining. I missed stimulating contacts with other adults and soon found that I was getting quite depressed. I decided there was no use feeling guilty for not being a full-time mother; and I became increasingly involved with the League of Women Voters, which I had joined the previous year and which, for the first time, was offering me stimulating and challenging volunteer activities.

As I became increasingly recognized for my civic work, Maurie, for the first time in our married life, became noticeably depressed despite his increasing stature in the medical community. (About this time he was elected president of the Iowa Dermatological Society.) I failed to realize that this depression probably stemmed from Maurie's concern that he was becoming eclipsed by my achievements. We were also facing difficulties because of our differing ideas about child rearing. He couldn't accept the fact that Susan wasn't the perfect child who would fulfill all his dreams and I felt his expectations for her were too high. In the fall of 1952 when I sought help from Dr. Sidney Sands, a Des Moines psychiatrist, Maurie felt very threatened. I think he sensed that this was a move toward greater independence on my part. He told me that all I needed was fifty cents worth of hormones (this was certainly a sexist diagnosis). Two days later he tripped over Susie's kitten and broke his pelvis. At that time treatment for a broken pelvis was to keep the patient in bed for six weeks. This meant that I was tied down taking care of Maurie. As I look back, I wonder if this accident might have been an unconscious effort to get my undivided attention.

With Sidney Sands's help, I started to explore what I really wanted out of life. This was a long and often painful process but invaluable in helping me determine who I was and in boosting my self-esteem. I had always considered my marriage commitment a lasting one but after several years I finally concluded that the best solution for me was to leave Maurie and strike out on my own. However, I decided that I would do nothing as long as Susan was still at home. About eight months after her marriage in June 1966, I finally made the break. This took a good deal of courage because at that time wives didn't leave their husbands; it was usually the other way around. I was lucky because I was economically independent. Maurie felt humiliated and abandoned when I left him and went around asking people to persuade me to come back. So that Maurie could get used to my absence and I could escape from the pressures to return home, I decided to go to Mexico for a few weeks. When I came back from Mexico, I settled down in the Americana Court Apartments with a sense of freedom and exhilaration, happy to be on my own at last. Maurie and I were divorced in the spring of 1969, and soon after, he announced his intention of marrying again. I was happy to know of his prospects for renewed happiness. About six o'clock in the morning in early September, I received a telephone call from Susan. "Daddy died last night," she told me. She explained that he had suffered a sudden heart attack. I lay there in bed, almost paralyzed by this news. I wondered if I could ever dare show my face in Des Moines again. I felt that the people who had been critical of me for leaving Maurie would now be blaming me for his death. An hour after Susan's call, I received a call from my friend, Mike Ball, telling me how sorry he was about Maurie's death. I realized then that I still had caring friends and Mike's call gave me the courage to get up and face the world. I was never more grateful for my supportive friends than I was that day. I soon found that life does go on. Now few people remember me as the former wife of Maurie Noun.

6

LEAGUE OF WOMEN VOTERS

Little did I know when I joined the League of Women Voters in 1944 that this organization would mark a distinct turning point in my life. The intellectual challenges which it brought me as well as the opportunity for meaningful action in the community met a need which had not been filled elsewhere. Yet I was not enthusiastic about joining the League. When Alice Polk, a neighbor my mother's age who was a member of a pioneer Des Moines family, called and asked me to come to an organizational meeting I told her that I was not interested. At this time of my life I really didn't know what I wanted and the easy way out seemed to be to make no commitments at all. But Alice insisted. Women, she told me, were obligated to carry their share of civic responsibility. In later years, when Alice was in a retirement home, I went to call on her. Thinking it would interest her to hear about my research into the history of women's suffrage in Iowa, I started to tell her of the book I was planning to write. She interrupted me to say that she had never been in favor of giving women the vote because they would not take their responsibility as voters seriously. It is evident that Alice's purpose in promoting the League of Women Voters was to make women responsible voters now that they had obtained a goal which she had opposed. I had always assumed that women I knew would be in favor of women voting, especially those connected with the League. I was amazed to find that here was a woman who belonged in my history of woman suffrage as one of the enemies.

Although I was not particularly interested in the League of Women Voters, I had been aware of its existence for many years. The national League was founded in 1919 at the suggestion of Carrie Chapman Catt, the Iowan who headed the National American Woman Suffrage Association during its final drive for ratification of the nineteenth amendment. When victory was in sight Chapman Catt recommended that women form a nonpartisan organization both to educate themselves as voters and to unite in using the vote for the common good regardless of party affiliation. During its early years the League supported a long list of issues relating to peace, maternal and child welfare, education, and the structure of government. Later the League shortened its agenda, realizing that there was a limit to the number of issues which it could deal with effectively. However the League's area of interests has remained essentially the same over the years. The Iowa League was founded in the early 1920s with Mother's friend, Flora Dunlap, as president. The Des Moines chapter was organized at about the same time. I can recall that there was a national League convention in Des Moines in 1923 and that my sister, Ruth, was assigned to chauffeur Belle Sherwin, a national officer, to various meetings. Sherwin's personal abilities must have been substantial but she is memorable to me because she was a member of the family which manufactured Sherwin-Williams paint. Mother would have liked Ruth, who had just graduated from college, to carry on as an active League member but Ruth was not interested.

The Des Moines League did good work for a number of years but gradually evolved into a Republican organization, and its charter was revoked in the early 1940s because it had lost its nonpartisan stance. The purpose of the meeting to which I was invited in 1944 was to form a successor organization. There was a small group present, probably no more than ten or fifteen women, none of whom had been associated with the former League. Helping with the organizational work was Margaret Strong, a League member from Grinnell who had taken the lead in disfranchising the former Des Moines chapter, and Edith Leopold, a League member from Burlington. Edith, a small, vivacious woman told us she was active in the League because she wanted a better world for her grandchildren. I must have been impressed with the idealism of the group because I consented to be treasurer of the Des Moines chapter which was organized that day. Balancing books, even for a very small organization, proved to be a frustrating job for me and I have never again been treasurer of any organization. Lami Gittler was chosen president because she was familiar with League work from her involvement with a League chapter at the University of Georgia where her husband had taught before coming to teach at Drake University. Gittler, a young woman with dark hair in braids wound around her head, was a natural teacher who led us step by step into League program and procedures. (At that time she had an infant daughter, Josie, who later became the first female member of the University of Iowa Law School faculty.) I can't remember what we studied in the two years Lami was president but I do know that in spite of disliking my job as treasurer, League activity heightened my interest in economic and social issues and was far more stimulating than any of the service-oriented volunteering that I had done in the past. The League also brought me into contact with women with whom I shared common interests and concerns and some of these women have remained close friends over the years.

When the new Des Moines League was organized, Margaret Strong announced that it was time that Des Moines help support the state League. I agreed to help her solicit local businesses and we were successful in raising several hundred dollars. I can vividly remember, however, my discomfort in raising money for an organization which had no record of action in the community. Furthermore, we didn't even have plans for future projects. This state of affairs did not last long. In 1947 the Des Moines League, under the leadership of Dolly Ratner, another relative newcomer to the city, decided to publish a book titled *You Are Democracy* that would describe the structure of government in Des Moines, Polk County, and the state as a whole. We planned to distribute copies free of charge to every home in the city. We estimated that we would need 50,000 copies, which would cost $10,000. This was an ambitious project for an organization with a small membership. My cousin, Babette Frankel, agreed to head the drive to raise the $10,000. I solicited as a team with Kay Stroud, an articulate and energetic person who took the lead in presenting our case when we called on prospects. Our most memorable contributor was the man who kept us in his office for a seemingly endless time telling us how he disapproved of women voting. He finally gave us $10.00. When the League had gotten 131 pledges totaling $7,500 we seemed to have exhausted all our potential resources. I offered to go to the Junior League with a proposal of joint sponsorship if they would contribute $2,500. This offer was accepted by the Junior League and so with their help the project went forward. The Junior League was particularly helpful in the house-to-house distribution of the book. *You Are Democracy*, edited by Betty Turner and Tolusa Cook, was a well-written and professional-looking publication. It was a project that established the Des Moines League of Women Voters as a responsible and worthwhile organization.

Having distributed a book describing Des Moines city government, the League of Women Voters soon set to work to make this book out of date. We did so by leading a campaign to drop the commission form of government, under which the city was currently operating, in favor of the council-manager plan. At this time Iowa law provided for three forms of municipal government. The first of these was the mayor-council form of government under which a mayor is elected at large and council persons are elected from wards. Des Moines had operated under the mayor-council form of government (with the council elected on a partisan basis) from the time of its incorporation in 1857 until 1908, when this system was rejected because it had become highly political, graft-ridden, and corrupt. The second form of government set forth in the state code was the nonpartisan commission form which provided for a council of five members, all of whom are elected at large. Each commissioner headed a department of city government—public affairs (the mayor), public safety, finance, parks, and public works. As a group the commissioners acted as policymakers for the city council; individually, they acted as administrators of their various departments. This form of government was considered more advantageous than the mayor-council system when it was adopted by Des Moines in 1908 because the council would be chosen on a nonpartisan basis, reduced in size, and elected by the city as a whole rather than by individual wards. This was supposed to lead to more unified government. In fact, commission government proved to be very unsatisfactory because each commissioner had his (and in one or two cases, her) own bailiwick and not even the mayor had any control over the individual departments. There was no overall coordination of budgeting or work so that vote trading, waste, and inefficiency resulted. The third form of municipal government provided for in the state code was the council-manager plan under which a nonpartisan council of five members is elected at large. These five choose one of their number as mayor. The council, in turn, hires an experienced and trained manager to run the city. The job of council members, considered to be part-time, is to set policies to be carried out by the manager. The League of Women Voters and other reform-minded citizens preferred the council-manager plan because it would take city administration out of the hands of amateurs and put it on a professional basis while still maintaining citizen control of municipal policies. By 1947 there was great dissatisfaction with commission government. The city was suffering from bad street maintenance, poor garbage collection, poor police protection, and a declining quality of municipal services. The current safety commissioner, Myron J. Bennett, a scoundrel popularly known as MJB, had his own piped-in music system that he sold to bars around town. This was a form of blackmail of those who unlawfully sold liquor. MJB also had a daily radio program on station KSO in which he freely promoted his own interests. Roy Miller, director of the Des Moines Tax Payers Association, was leading a movement to call a referendum on the question of adopting the council-manager type of government. League members were eager to help with this effort.

In the spring of 1948 I agreed to become president of the League with the understanding that Charlotte Robling, the current president, would head the League's council-manager campaign efforts. Later that spring I attended the national convention of the League of Women Voters at Grand Rapids, Michigan. This convention, with its hundreds of women earnestly debating public issues under strict parliamentary rules, was a new and impressive experience for me. I visited with Leaguers from Hartford, Connecticut, and other communities which had recently had successful campaigns for council-manager government and I arrived home full of enthusiasm about launching a campaign in Des Moines.

About this time, however, a field worker from the national League of Women Voters came to visit us and was appalled at our failure to follow the established League procedure of presenting subjects to the membership for study and then letting them decide what kind of action, if any, they wanted to take on a particular issue. I can recall spending an entire afternoon at a board meeting at Bobby Fox's home listening to the field worker go point by point over a manual describing how a local league should operate. Since we were a new and enthusiastic League, I didn't feel too guilty about our lack of attention to proper procedures but we did set about mending our ways. During the summer the League organized study groups to educate members about council-manager government. (My guess is that there were about fifty members at this time.) A poll of the membership in November indicated an almost unanimous desire to work for a referendum on a change of form of government. At the same time the League took a survey of how the council-manager system was working in seventy-seven communities. We wrote to a variety of persons, including labor leaders, city officials, and business persons. With the exception of one or two labor groups we got very favorable replies. Using these reports, Dolly Ratner's husband, Jay, editor of *Better Homes and Gardens*, made an impressive flip chart for use in public presentations.

Meanwhile, a Citizens' Committee for Council-Manager Government was formed and efforts were made to unite various elements of the city in supporting the plan. It soon became evident, however, that organized labor, which was much stronger in 1948 than it is today, would oppose a referendum for a change of government. Labor had very friendly relations with the current public works commissioner and was afraid of losing its influence if the job were put into professional hands. In addition, labor feared that a part-time council under the council-manager plan would be dominated by business interests unsympathetic to their cause. I was dismayed when Charlotte Robling, the person I was relying on to head the League's work in the council-manager campaign, came to me late in the fall and announced that she was so sympathetic to labor's point of view that she was resigning from her job. Fortunately Kay Stroud was willing to step into the breach.

The League formally kicked off the council-manager campaign in the fall of 1948 with a luncheon at Hotel Fort Des Moines. We were pleased with a large turnout, but I was terrified at the thought of presiding at a meeting of this kind. So I arranged to have Kay take over my duties. My only job was to introduce Kay. This was the first time I had ever used a microphone and I was so nervous I can still feel the reverberations of that mike as I made the introduction. Jay Ratner presented our flip chart along with an explanation of the merits of council-manager government and the campaign seemed to be off to a good start. My brother, Joe, raised $10,000 to help finance the campaign and Kay was hired to manage the campaign office.

It soon became evident, however, that this was not going to be an easy campaign. City employees, fearful of change, were united in opposing the referendum. Businessmen, unwilling to make enemies of organized labor, took cover. With few exceptions, we women were left to carry the load. Iowa law at that time provided that in order to call a referendum, petitions needed to be signed by 10 percent of the voters in each of Des Moines' two townships. There was no trouble getting the required number of signatures in the township on the west side of the city, but voters in Lee Township on the east side, traditionally hostile to the more prosperous west side, and fearful of the business interests which favored council-manager government, proved to be a serious stumbling block. Even those east-side residents who favored the referendum were hesitant about signing a petition because of fear of retaliation from those who opposed it. The campaign soon boiled down to an east side versus west side battle. Our difficulties were further complicated by one of the worst winters

Des Moines had ever experienced. In addition to the extreme cold, the ground was covered with a glassy layer of ice and snow which made walking very hazardous. Despite these drawbacks, League women trudged from house to house on the east side day after day, often coming back with as few as two or three signatures. Finally, by early spring we secured a sufficient number of signatures to be able to force the city council to call an election, which they set for April 30. This was Drake Relays day and the council hoped the attraction of the relays would diminish interest in the election. It was also a Saturday, when laboring people had more time to vote.

The delay in filing petitions had given us ample time for an educational campaign. Public speaking was still too frightening for me so I confined my efforts to talking to small, informal groups such as high school classes. Kay Stroud and others spoke to larger audiences and debated the issues before groups which did not want to "take sides." I did agree to be on a radio call-in program with Kay and my trepidation wasn't helped by Mother, who warned me that my enunciation was so poor that probably no one would understand me. Nonetheless, this, my first radio appearance (there was no television at that time) proved to be a great success. Kay and I were easily able to answer all the questions that came in. Finally, a man called and said, "You women know a lot about city government but can either of you bake a cake?" This was long before the feminist movement had arrived to make me feisty about such put downs, so Kay and I proceeded to praise each other's cooking. That man would have gotten a different answer today.

Our most vocal opponent during the campaign was MJB, the safety commissioner who used his daily radio program to blast the council-manager plan in general and the women who were working in the campaign in particular. When our patience had worn thin, a letter of complaint to the Federal Communications Commission was sent under my name asking if the commission didn't think we deserved equal time. The day before the referendum (April 29, 1949), the *Iowa Federationist*, a labor paper whose principal writer was Russ Lavine, a right-wing agitator, came out with a story headed, "MANAGER PLAN MRS. NOUN HITS FREE SPEECH: ASKS MJB BE PUT OFF AIR." "Opponents of the manager plan," the story said, "have pointed to it as undemocratic and un-American. As a proponent of the plan, Mrs. Noun seems to adhere to some of these principles, mainly against the 'right of free speech.'" This story was picked up in its entirety by station KSO and repeated at intervals all during the day. I protested to the station, demanding a retraction of the accusation that I had asked MJB be put off the air. The station continued broadcasting the charges against me, followed by a brief statement saying that I denied them. This was my first experience in dealing with hostile public media and I learned the hard way that a denial of widely disseminated material does little to rectify the situation.

Ten days before the election Richard Childs, a mild-mannered gentleman in his late sixties, known as the father of the council-manager form of government, came to Des Moines to help us out. Childs, an officer of the National Municipal League, was dedicated to the cause of municipal reform. Kay Stroud and I kept Childs busy for a full day with meetings and interviews. In the evening he took part in a debate at East High School before an unfriendly audience of over a thousand people with police stationed at every entranceway. Childs seemed truly out of place in this hostile atmosphere and his gentlemanly manner of speaking was no match for his aggressive opponents on the platform. When Childs got back to New York he reported to his office that we were beaten in Des Moines. Nonetheless, he was deeply impressed with "the kind of courage that led those League leaders to plug doggedly ahead, alone and almost deserted, through the darkening prospect." (Speech to the La Guardia Memorial Association, Dec. 13, 1958, at the Astor Hotel, New York City, at its Eighth Annual Award to the LWV of the United States)

Probably because of our inexperience, we Leaguers were hopeful about the outcome of the election, despite the seeming odds against us. My heart sank, however, when I watched the vote being counted at a precinct in the Roadside district, a poor area on the east side. The votes were almost solidly against us. At a gathering of campaign workers at my house later that evening, prospects for success looked brighter as returns from friendly precincts came in. Finally, Kay and I were able to send Childs a telegram saying, "Des Moines adopts manager plan by 880 majority in 44,000 votes. Ain't that something?" Childs's reply, intended as highly complementary, read, "You gorgeous girls!" At this time my feminist consciousness was so undeveloped that I didn't stop to think how sexist the term *girl* is when applied to a mature woman.

The *Des Moines Tribune* (May 3, 1949) gave the women full credit for this narrow victory in an editorial titled, "THE WOMEN, BLESS 'EM!" It went on to say, "The real fight . . . was between the 'ins' as represented by the city council and many city workers and their allies among the labor union leaders on one side, against an assortment of ordinary citizens and young idealists on the other side. Most of these young idealists were women—still in some ways an 'oppressed'

class . . . who did most of the work. . . . Women as WOMEN are a neg-
ligible factor in politics. But when a group of them organizes and
works on a project that appeals to the good sense of the WHOLE
COMMUNITY, they can put it over—even against formidable opposition. . . ." In other words, if women work hard for a cause with wide
community support they can be successful, but otherwise, the editorial infers, women had better not try.

As a result of our work in the council-manager campaign, the Des
Moines League received the Lane Bryant award of $1,000, for out-
standing community service in the United States. I represented the
League at the award ceremonies, which were held at a luncheon at
the swank Plaza Hotel in New York in November 1950, with such
notables as Margaret Mead in the audience. This award received extensive publicity with stories and pictures in New York papers, including the *New York Times*, the *World Telegram*, the *Mirror*, and the
Herald Tribune, as well as in our own *Des Moines Register*. As a result
of our work for reform government, membership in the Des Moines
League more than doubled and the League was now looked upon as
an effective force in the city.

My year as president of the League was a landmark year in my
life. For the first time, I was not a follower but a leader and as I look
back, the withdrawal of the active support of the business community meant more experience and more leadership roles for women.
We were free to conduct the council-manager campaign with little or
no interference from males who usually took the lead in such projects. I learned a lot about municipal government, about how to conduct a political campaign, and about how to keep an organization
running smoothly. The campaign also gave me my first experience as
a public person. During this period I wrote my first letters to the Des
Moines papers concerning political issues, I appeared on my first
radio program, and I first spoke in front of a microphone from a public platform. From my first brief introduction of Kay Stroud at the
luncheon kicking off the council-manager campaign to my nervous
acceptance speech at the Lane Bryant luncheon in New York I traveled a difficult road. However, these were invaluable experiences in
helping me get used to speaking in public. My painful shyness and
lack of self-esteem no doubt played a large part in my fear of speaking. But as I gradually became convinced that I had something worthwhile to say I became more confident. By the time the council-
manager campaign was over I was on my way, but it took several
years before I began to feel any degree of confidence when speaking
in public.

The euphoria caused by the council-manager victory ended when I found that after the women had done the hard work, the men were taking over. Harold Brenton, a banker who had stayed under cover during the campaign, organized a Good Government Committee to select a slate of candidates for the first city council under the council-manager plan. The election was to be held in the fall of 1950. League leaders were not invited to join this committee. What was particularly galling was the fact that Newton Margulies, a leading opponent of council-manager government, was co-chair of this committee. The unspoken message seemed to be that now that the women had done their good work, they should go quietly home and let the men take over the important job of running the city. As women we were neither psychologically nor politically able to challenge Brenton's committee. On the other hand, we were not willing to be ignored. Kay Stroud, who had succeeded me as president of the Des Moines League, went to Brenton and demanded that I be put on the committee. He acceded to her request. Women were allotted five memberships on Brenton's twenty-two-member committee. At committee meetings Brenton let everyone express him- or herself freely but I always had the feeling that what we said made very little difference. He and a few of his male cohorts made the final decisions. The committee eventually endorsed a full slate for the five-member council, including two representatives from labor and one woman. I helped the League of Women Voters organize an ambitious "get out the vote" project for this first election under the council-manager plan. We recruited women in every precinct to be at the polls on election day to present a gold feather to everyone who voted. One of the labor men had a stroke shortly before the election and because of his illness was defeated. The other four candidates were elected.

I soon became involved in another aspect of municipal government when I undertook a study of home rule in Iowa for the state League of Women Voters. This interest in home rule was generated by Corbet Long, assistant to Leonard Howell, the newly appointed city manager, who complained about how hampered the city of Des Moines was because of the lack of home rule powers for cities and towns in Iowa. Municipalities could not act in any area without specific authority having been granted by the legislature. What was needed, Long said, was state legislation permitting cities and towns to operate unrestrictedly in purely local matters as long as they did not conflict with Iowa law. The Des Moines League of Women Voters, anxious to carry on with local government reform, persuaded the state League at its 1951 convention to make a study of home rule. The study would be used as background for consideration of adopting the issue as an action item at its next annual convention. I agreed to make the study and spent most of the next year studying textbooks on state and local government, reading the Iowa Code, and researching the history of municipal government in Iowa. My family heard so much about home rule that my seven-year-old daughter, confusing home rule with home room, asked me if I would be a home rule mother! The home rule study was a great educational experience for me and received high commendation from Corbett Long. Long wrote, "It is an excellent job and one that makes us full-time specialists aware that we aren't such specialists after all." John Bebout of the National Municipal League thought it was so good that it should be printed in pamphlet form for use in schools. Subsequently, I arranged for the Iowa League of Municipalities to publish the study in its monthly magazine (December 1952) and to make a quantity of reprints available for wider distribution. But, alas, members of the League of Women Voters outside of Des Moines were not interested in home rule. The state League, at its next convention, voted to drop the issue from its agenda. Leaguers living in the smaller cities and towns of the state had not yet felt a compelling need for this kind of enabling legislation. To my knowledge, this is the only time that the Iowa League has refused to take action on an item which it had adopted for study. I was disappointed that the League did not go ahead with action on the home rule study but it was evident that there was little interest in the subject. Twenty years later the Iowa legislature did enact a home rule law. I took quiet satisfaction in seeing the Iowa League of Women Voters support this legislation.

The initiation of the council-manager plan in Des Moines did not mean the end of opposition to this form of municipal government. The most prominent spokesperson for the opposition was Russ Lavine, right-wing radio-talk-show host and writer for labor's organ, the *Federationist*. In 1959 Lavine and his cohorts were successful in getting enough petition signatures to force a referendum to drop council-manager government in favor of the mayor-council form. Instead of a small council elected at large, this form of government called for a much larger council elected from wards and did away with the position of city manager. Des Moines had dropped this form of government in 1908. Once again, the League of Women Voters was active in defending the manager plan but this time there was substantial help from the business community. My main contribution to this campaign was researching and writing a paper on the history of municipal government in Des Moines, showing how poorly the mayor-council system had worked in the past. I also spoke at a meeting at North High School. To this inexperienced speaker the crowd seemed like thousands but the *Des Moines Register* reported an audience of about 250. To those who didn't know me well, I may have seemed quite self-possessed, but my fourteen-year-old daughter, Susan, who was very sensitive to my signs of nervousness noticed that my voice quavered. Since that time she has judged the success of my public speaking by the steadiness of my voice.

I also wrote a lengthy letter to the *Des Moines Register* (June 8, 1959) pointing out the weaknesses of mayor-council-ward government and asking if Des Moines wanted to go back to the extravagant, wasteful, and graft-ridden kind of government which it had given up fifty years ago. This brought a prompt reply from Russ Lavine in the *Federationist* (June 12, 1959) in which he said, "If Mrs. N. feels that the people of Des Moines are such morons, that they are incapable of self-government, then she should submit to a decontamination chamber and take her chastity elsewhere." In the referendum which was held on June 23, 1959, the manager plan was endorsed by more than 63 percent of those voting. This margin was far greater than the tiny majority with which the plan had skimped through ten years previously. But this did not mean the end of attacks on council-manager government. The same people who had originally opposed adoption of the plan continued to work for its abandonment.

The League of Women Voters finally came to the conclusion that the size and composition of the city council must be changed to satisfy some of the demands of opponents if Des Moines were to be spared the continuing threat of losing council-manager government. The League helped work for a state law that gave Des Moines a chance to modify the council-manager system by enlarging the council to seven members, four of whom were to be elected from districts, and three, including the mayor, to be elected at large. The business community and the *Des Moines Register* and the *Des Moines Tribune* opposed this change. They feared that election by wards would make for a divisive city government; also that it would make it easier for opponents of council-manager government to be elected to the council. The League concluded that the three members elected at large would usually hold the balance of power even if an opponent or two of council-manager government were elected from wards. A referendum on this modification was approved by Des Moines voters in the fall of 1967. In a letter of support of the change that was published in the *Des Moines Register* prior to the election (June 8, 1959), I predicted, "Despite dire warnings of disaster by Jeremiahs who oppose this change, . . . [this] modification of the size and composition of our City Council . . . may be the means by which the council-manager plan itself will be saved from defeat in future elections." Since Des Moines has had the seven-member council, there has never been a challenge to the council-manager form of government. As James Flansburg of the *Des Moines Register* has commented, this plan "plugged the gadflies into the system giving them a chance to make it work"*

The contacts I made with the National Municipal League during the campaign for council-manager government in 1949 led to my election as a member of the council of the Municipal League in 1951. At the League's annual conference on government in Memphis, Tennessee, in 1956, I was both surprised and pleased to be awarded the League's distinguished citizen award. This citation reads: "A modest novice who entered the civic arena of Des Moines, she worked with fellow citizens to oust a shabby municipal administration and install the council-manager plan; now in the continuing defense against scurrilous counter-attacks, she is a true guardian of good government and a volunteer worker for sound education for citizenship." The printed form to which this citation is attached and on which my name is inscribed commends the recipient "For his faithful service to the community" and "his self-sacrificing efforts to make a reality of self-government." I trust that since that time the Municipal League has found a more appropriate form to fill out for award recipients who are female.

In honor of my honor, the Des Moines League of Women Voters presented me with a bunch of red roses, and more importantly, a thoughtful tribute praising me for my "modesty, my calm approach to a problem in the midst of turmoil, and my thoughts always of the future and never looking back." An editorial in the *Des Moines Tribune* on November 15, 1956, called my honor "deserved recognition," and went on to comment, "Mrs. Noun is representative of many women who make intelligent and unselfish contributions toward the cause of good local government. They don't aspire to political careers nor do they expect any reward in the way of business or professional advancement. . . . They work through their organizations for reforms and changes they think will benefit the city."

If the truth were known, there were a number of us "unselfish" women who would have liked to run for political office. But no one asked us to and we didn't have the courage to do so without the

Des Moines Register, Dec. 12, 1981.

endorsement of the Good Government Committee or some other influential group. As women we were doing what we were supposed to do—being civic-minded volunteers and letting the men run the show. At this time there was no women's movement to encourage us to run for office and to give us backing in our campaigns. We just accepted the fact that running for office was generally not in the cards for us. At a meeting of the National Municipal League in Richmond, Virginia, in 1953, I was part of a panel that discussed "Women as Campaigners." I pointed out that women were better reformers than men because they were in the home and therefore not afraid to press for unpopular causes out of fear of losing their jobs. In retrospect this kind of reasoning seems pretty antediluvian. My thinking at this time was that reform was the province of college-educated, non-wage-earning women working as volunteers without any thought of seeking public office. I not only ignored the fact that millions of women were not full-time homemakers but also the fact that men usually hold the ultimate power and that without their backing the goals of reform-minded women would be difficult to achieve. Further evidence of my undeveloped feminism was my agreement with the conclusion of this panel that female candidates for public office should be "young and attractive enough to appeal to men."* This statement indicates the lack of feminist consciousness of all eleven women on the panel. In fact, we were just buying into the stereotype of women's need to be young and beautiful in order to be successful rather than emphasizing that women are just as capable of holding public office as men and that they should be judged on their merits and not their looks.

Finally, in the spring of 1973 I became courageous enough to explore the possibility of running for one of the at-large seats on the city council against Russ Lavine, the radio-talk-show host who had so bitterly opposed the adoption of council-manager government and who continued to be a leading critic of city government. Ever since I had taken part in the campaign for council-manager government I had secretly desired to run for the city council. However, I didn't have the courage to step forward and offer myself as a candidate and no one asked me to run. The idea of opposing Lavine appealed to me and I thought I would have a good chance of defeating him. I figured that I needed the support of the business community to be successful but the men I consulted told me I was too controversial and advised me not to run. At this time I was active in the feminist movement, which

*Richmond Times-Dispatch, Nov. 11, 1953.

was not looked on with favor by the male establishment, and I was also well known for my involvement with the Iowa Civil Liberties Union, which often defended the rights of people associated with unpopular causes. Also, the fact that I was an independent-minded woman didn't enhance my popularity with the business community. Even my brother, Joe, discouraged my candidacy. I didn't have the courage to run for office without the backing of the business establishment, so I decided that I would just keep on working for controversial causes. The men backed one of their own, Bill Reichardt, a popular former football star. Ironically, Reichardt was soundly defeated by Lavine. I must admit that I took a secret delight in this turn of events. While Lavine would never have been my choice to hold a seat on the city council, the fact that he was in a position of responsibility made him so much a part of the system that he stopped sniping at council actions. He also ceased to agitate for change in the form of city government.

One of the most important issues tackled by the Iowa League of Women Voters in the 1950s and 1960s was a drive to reapportion the Iowa legislature. At this time the House of Representatives was composed of one representative from each county with an additional representative from each of the nine largest counties. This meant that a county with a population of 10,000 had one representative while Polk County, with a population of 200,000, had only two representatives. The Senate was composed of fifty members elected from districts. There could only be one senator from each district. The result was that the senator from Polk County (which was designated a district) represented 200,000 people while senators from other districts represented as few as 25,000 people. Since the rural areas would never voluntarily give up their power over more populous districts, it was unlikely that the legislature would reapportion itself. In spite of the obvious unfairness of the situation, reapportionment was also opposed by organizations as disparate as the Iowa Manufacturers Association and the Iowa Farm Bureau Federation. Neither group wanted to lose the influence which it had under the present system.

A constitutional convention with delegates apportioned according to population seemed to offer one possible way out of this quagmire. Iowa law requires that there be a question regarding calling a constitutional convention on the ballot every ten years. Since 1960 was the year for such a referendum, the League sought to educate voters about important reforms that such a convention might achieve. These included judicial reform, strengthening the office of the governor, and, most importantly, reapportionment. As part of this effort, Marguerite Neff and I organized a conference, "Focus on Iowa's Constitution," which was held at the Savery Hotel in Des Moines in April 1960. We drew an overflow audience and the meeting was a great success. Despite the enthusiastic support for a constitutional convention on the part of the League and other supporters of reapportionment, the general public was apathetic. This apathy, combined with active opposition by groups such as the Iowa Farm Bureau Federation and the Iowa Manufacturers Association, resulted in a negative vote on the referendum in the fall election.

The U. S. Supreme Court came to the rescue in the 1960s with a series of decisions which indicated that both houses of state legislatures must be apportioned according to population and that the districts must be as nearly equal as possible. Prodded by these decisions, the Iowa legislature agreed to an amendment to the Iowa constitution which provided for reapportionment that met Supreme Court standards. This amendment was approved by the voters in 1968. But the reapportionment plan adopted by the next general assembly still left districts with a population variance of 3.8 percent and it was gerrymandered in favor of Republican incumbents.

This plan was challenged in a suit filed in the Iowa Supreme Court by the Iowa League of Women Voters, the Democratic party, and me as an individual. At this time I was president of the Iowa Civil Liberties Union and Dan Johnston, lawyer for the plaintiffs, thought my name and title would be helpful even though the Civil Liberties Union as an organization was not involved. In April 1972 the Court declared the legislature's reapportionment plan unconstitutional and substituted a plan of its own that provided for districts with a population deviance of less than 1 percent. My part in this reapportionment victory was minor compared with other Leaguers but it was satisfying to be a part of such a successful campaign.

An important part of my League education came during the infamous McCarthy era in the early 1950s. I joined a League study group on the Bill of Rights based on a series of booklets published by the national League of Women Voters. Senator Joseph McCarthy had sparked a virulent anti-Communist witch-hunt which was sweeping the country and causing dozens of innocent people to be called to testify before the House Un-American Activities Committee. Emotions were high on the part of those who were either pro- or anti-McCarthy. An indication of the temper of the times came from Dr. Mary Hunter, a resident of an old people's home, who was a member of our study group. As I helped her to my car after a meeting at which we discussed First Amendment rights, she remarked, "I can tell you, there is no freedom of speech where I live." In retrospect, I realize that while we earnestly studied the Bill of Rights during the McCarthy era, we did not feel impelled to take any action to counter the current hysteria. Such action would no doubt have branded us as part of the Communist conspiracy.

Ironically, it was a civil rights issue—the refusal of the Des Moines League to take a firm stand against racial discrimination in housing—that eventually made me decide that the League was too conservative, if not actually racist in its attitudes, for me to continue as an active member. Although in the early 1950s the League voted to support the establishment of a fair employment practices commission in Des Moines, in the early 1960s Pauline Millen and I met determined opposition when we tried to get the League to work against discrimination in housing because of race. At the annual meeting of the League in 1962, we offered a motion to include a study of segregated housing as part of an overall study of low-cost housing in Des Moines. Faced with taking a pubic stand on the issue of fair housing, this meeting—after much hesitation—went on record with the mild statement that the League "does not favor racial segregation in housing in Des Moines." However, nothing was done during the following year to implement this position, and the next annual meeting refused to commit the League to any action in this area. It was evident that while League members were favorable to elimination of discrimination because of race in employment, which was unlikely to affect them personally, they didn't want their neighborhoods opened to minorities. Even the League president told me that she wouldn't want a black living next door to her. The civil rights movement was at its height at this time and it seemed inexcusable to me that the League would want to ignore an important issue like fair housing for minorities. It made me realize that the League, as a middle-of-the-road organization, too often ducks controversial issues relating to civil rights, civil liberties, and (with the exception of the ERA) even women's rights. The League works best for more socially acceptable reforms related to the structure of government such as the council-manager plan, reapportionment, and electing the governor and lieutenant governor on a single ticket.

In reviewing my work with the League of Women Voters I am impressed with all the opportunities the League gave me for education about local, state, and national government as well as for the opportunities it offered for community service and personal development. My League work not only broadened my intellectual horizons but also helped build my confidence in conducting meetings and speaking in public. The League opened a new world for me, far different from the service-oriented volunteerism I had previously known, and gave me invaluable experience in working with an activist organization. In addition to all I learned through the League, I am especially grateful for the lifelong friendships I made during my years as an active member. ⟍

Just as I finished the above paragraphs I received in the mail the latest issue of the *Metro Voter*, the publication of the Des Moines League of Women Voters.* It carries a quotation from Maud Wood Park's address to the 1924 national League convention which pretty clearly explains my eventual frustration with the League. Park stated: "[The League] has chosen to be a middle-of-the-road organization in which persons of widely differing political views might work out together a program of definite advance on which they could agree. It has not sought to lead a few women a long way quickly but rather to lead many women a little way at a time. . . ." In retrospect, it seems to me that as I worked with the League I increasingly felt hemmed in by this middle-of-the-road philosophy as well as the League's slow and deliberate methods. I needed a wider and faster track than the League could offer me.

*October 1988, p. 4.

7

IOWA CIVIL LIBERTIES UNION

W hen I became president of the Iowa Civil Liberties Union in 1964 I was unaware that the next few years would bring forth a multitude of civil liberties issues, many caused by the war in Vietnam and the resulting student unrest. It was not long, however, before the tension between those who opposed the war and those who believed that the war was stopping the spread of communism in Southeast Asia had reached an almost hysterical pitch. The pro-war group looked on war protesters as unpatriotic. They feared that anti-war protests would lead to social disorder and violence and therefore should be suppressed. Although the Civil Liberties Union took no position on the war itself, we said that if protest could be reasonably defended as a constitutional right, then we would defend it. In 1969 Des Moines Mayor Tom Urban was so concerned about possible disorder on the streets that he refused to allow an antiwar demonstration sponsored by the Students for a Democratic Society to march through downtown Des Moines. Instead, the marchers had to take a circuitous three-mile route from Good Park to the State Capitol. I accompanied this march as an observer to monitor how the police handled the situation. The event went off quietly, in spite of the fact that the students expected violence on the part of the police, and the police expected the students to create a disturbance. When *Des Moines Register* columnist Don Kaul spoke at Spencer, Iowa, under the auspices of the northwest chapter of the ICLU, a saboteur pulled the master switch, which left the auditorium in total darkness. Kaul delivered his speech with the aid of a single spotlight. In a column reporting on this incident, Kaul commented that "the mood of the country today is ominous, made up of equal parts of paranoia, fear, and anger." The head of the American Legion said in a Des Moines speech that the ACLU should be investigated by the House Un-American Activities Committee. After reading about a talk that I had given at an Urbandale school, a woman called the teacher in charge and wanted equal time. She said I was part of "that international organization" and that the FBI had a dossier on me. The teacher assured her that there was no controversy in discussing the Bill of Rights that necessitated the "other" side's being represented. During this period I received a good deal of anonymous hate mail from people who were angered because the ICLU was defending people with unpopular points of view.

The most notable case handled by the ICLU during the Vietnam War was in defense of three children who were suspended from Des Moines schools in December 1965 because they wore black armbands to school to mourn the dead in Vietnam. The ICLU involvement with the armband case began when Leonard Tinker, peace education director for the American Friends Service Committee, called me one evening in mid-December to tell me his children and several others were planning to wear black armbands during the Christmas season and that school authorities had threatened to send the children home if they wore them to school. Tinker wanted to know if the ICLU would defend the kids if they were suspended. Although I couldn't give him a positive answer without consulting the board, I told Tinker I felt sure we would be supportive. Little did I know that this conversation was the beginning of the ICLU's involvement with a case which would eventually result in a landmark free speech decision by the Supreme Court of the United States. A day or two after my conversation with Tinker, his two children, John and Mary Beth, and another youngster, Christopher Eckhardt, did wear black armbands to school. They were sent home and told not to return until they had removed the armbands. This was shortly before Christmas vacation. Because their protest had been planned to last only during the holiday season the children did not wear the armbands when they returned to school after the first of the year. Meanwhile the controversy over the propriety of the school administration's attitude toward this expression of protest continued unabated.

Ora Niffeneger, president of the Board of Education, refused the request of students to call a special board meeting to discuss the armband issue. As far as he personally was concerned, the leaders of our country had decided on a course of action and they should be supported. The controversy erupted in full when the school board met in late December. Over two hundred people jammed the board room to express their views—both pro and con—on the subject. The ICLU was represented by Craig Sawyer, a volatile and abrasive Drake law professor. The ICLU took the position that students had a right to free expression, even expression of unpopular views, as long as they created no undue disturbance. Sawyer called for immediate reinstatement of the students and adoption of a policy approving all means of peaceable expression. When a board member moved to postpone a decision, Sawyer objected. "Take a stand! That's what you are here for," he demanded. The Board of Education, disregarding Sawyer's demand, voted to let the armband prohibition stand pending further study.

The next meeting of the Board of Education in early January was equally contentious. The board room was again packed with several hundred people anxious to express their views on the armband question. Board member Mary Grefe read a lengthy statement expressing her opinion that schoolchildren should obey school authorities and that it was the administration's duty to enforce regulations. She said a small group of parents should not use the schools as a vehicle for promoting their ideas and convictions. I represented the ICLU at this meeting because our board feared Sawyer was too abrasive. Val Schoenthal prepared a lengthy statement for me to present which expressed the ICLU position in firm but deferential terms. However, since my turn to speak did not come until near the end of the meeting, I got no further than a sentence or two when I was cut off for lack of time. (My statement and also Mary Grefe's were subsequently published in full in the Des Moines Tribune, January 5 and and 10, 1966.) The Board of Education at this time voted five to two to support the school administration in their rule against armbands.

I was indignant over the school board's action and saw the armband situation as a prime civil liberties issue. Dan Johnston, a recent graduate of Drake law school who was working part time as ICLU legal counsel, was willing to defend the children but felt he couldn't afford the time since he was just starting his law practice. My brother Joe and I offered to give Dan financial support if he would take the case for the ICLU. The trial was held in July 1966 before U.S. District Court Judge Roy Stephenson, with armband wearers Beth and John Tinker and Christopher Eckhardt as plaintiffs. I was impressed with the poise with which the children explained their position, and I thought the prosecution's case was very weak. There was no evidence that there had been any disturbance because of the armbands.

In addition, it was brought out that school policies were inconsistent in that the wearing of other controversial symbols, such as the Nazi swastika, were permitted. In spite of this evidence Stephenson ruled against the children on the basis that the armbands might have caused a disturbance and therefore a prohibition against them was not unreasonable. Stephenson, a Brigadier General with combat duty in World War II, was personally unsympathetic to this antiwar protest. He told Dan Johnston in private that he couldn't understand what the children wanted.

The 8th U.S. District Court of Appeals in St. Louis split four to four on the appeal and the U.S. Supreme Court subsequently agreed to review the case. I went to Washington to attend the Supreme Court hearing. Although Dan had received substantial help with his brief from the American Civil Liberties Union, the armband case was still his and as a young and relatively inexperienced lawyer, he was so nervous the night before the hearing that I wasn't sure he would make it to court the next day. However, he conducted himself with calm self-assurance during the trial, helped no doubt by the fact that he was facing a friendly court. The Court's ruling, which came down in February 1969, was a ringing victory for students' freedom of expression. Abe Fortas, who delivered the opinion for the Court, declared that although state-operated schools may be permitted reasonable regulation of speech-connected activities, they may not be enclaves of totalitarianism and that school officials do not possess absolute authority over students. Students, in school and out, are "persons" under our Constitution and freedom of speech does not stop at the schoolhouse door. The armband decision was a great victory for Dan and ICLU as well as for all public school students. It was a thrill for me to be a part of this victory.

In another war-related situation, the University of Iowa Board of Student Publications fired Leona Durham, editor of the *Daily Iowan*, in mid-May 1970 before she had published a single issue. Durham, a campus radical, was known to have taken part in recent antiwar street demonstrations. The board, which only a few weeks previously had hired Durham, panicked after four people were killed at Kent State University on May 4, 1970. They argued that because the campus was in turmoil, an inexperienced editor such as Durham could aggravate a touchy situation. The ICLU asked for an investigation of the firing. As a result, the Board of Student Publications appointed a commission of three to look into the situation and make recommendations. Durham chose me as her representative on the commission and the board chose John McCormally, editor of the

Burlington Hawkeye. The third member was Ronald Carlson, a law professor at the University of Iowa. The selection of McCormally by the Board of Publications seemed a naive choice, for McCormally was a well-known liberal who was not likely to support the board's position. The conservative *Waterloo Courier* commented that putting McCormally and Noun on this commission was comparable to appointing J. Edgar Hoover to investigate the FBI. The hearing on Durham's dismissal went on for almost three days and I was amazed at the parade of professors who defended the action of the board as necessary and correct. Especially remarkable were those who claimed membership in the ICLU while defending Durham's firing on the basis that her editorship might cause further campus disruption. The report of our commission, McCormally and I in the majority, recommended rehiring Durham without unreasonable delay. Durham was subsequently reinstated as editor and my reward for serving on the commission was a year's subscription to the *Daily Iowan*. The only "radical" element I could detect in Durham's editorship was a plethora of feminist articles, which were a welcome addition to the paper's editorial content.

The years I was involved with the ICLU were a time of growth and expanding horizons for me. Not only was I involved with basic issues of freedom which were of great concern to me but I was also working with people who were dedicated to these same values. I had been an inactive member of the American Civil Liberties Union and its local chapter, the Iowa Civil Liberties Union, for a number of years prior to my election to the ICLU board in 1961. At this time activities of the ICLU were at a low ebb. We met once a month at Bishop's cafeteria in downtown Des Moines, a popular low-cost restaurant with a balcony where a group could meet with a minimum of disturbance. We usually had an early supper followed by a short meeting and were on our way home in hardly more than an hour. We had no legal cases at this time and our activities were limited to passing resolutions and writing occasional letters on civil liberties issues. In 1962 when Kenneth Everhart, the current president of the ICLU, moved out of town the board asked Sidney Levine, a lawyer, if he would like to fill out Everhart's term as president. Sidney, although not a board member, was a frequent visitor at our meetings and was apparently very much interested in the organization. He was delighted to accept the position as president of the board but it soon became evident that he did little more than preside at meetings. Katherine Bertin, our devoted secretary, did her best to keep the ICLU from disintegrating, trying to rescue unanswered mail from Levine's office and seeing that membership records were kept current. Despite the organization's inactivity, I found satisfaction in my ICLU associations because they brought me into contact with liberals who took for granted a support of civil rights and civil liberties issues that I had not found in the League of Women Voters. While the League had shied away from the issue of racial discrimination in housing, the ICLU had me testify before the city's Equal Opportunity Committee asking for "teeth" in the Des Moines fair-housing ordinance regarding discrimination because of race.

I undertook my first real task as an ICLU board member in the fall of 1963 when Don Murphy asked me to help him get out an issue of the *Defender*, the bulletin of the ICLU. Don, a long-time, very devoted member of the ICLU, was a brilliant journalist who was editor of the monthly journal *Wallace's Farmer*. He had undertaken responsibility for the *Defender* for a number of years but he was now suffering from Parkinson's disease and needed help. I had no idea what to put in the bulletin for there was little ICLU news to report but Don promised that he would furnish me with editorial material if I would see to makeup, printing, and distribution. In the material Don provided me was a story about how to celebrate Christmas in the schools in an acceptably nonreligious manner. Hymns containing reference to "Our Lord Jesus Christ" should not be sung but it was all right to sing "Deck the Halls," or "We Wish You a Merry Christmas." My friends Jeanette Eyerly, a devout Catholic, and her husband Frank, editor of the *Des Moines Register*, were so indignant that the Civil Liberties Union would want to take the religious meaning out of school Christmas celebrations that they promptly resigned as ICLU members. Frank continued to be a critic of the ICLU for all my active years with the organization.

In early 1964 I was approached by ICLU board members Don Murphy, Gil Cranberg, an editorial writer for the *Des Moines Register*, and Val Schoenthal, a member of a prominent Des Moines law firm, with the request that I take over the presidency of the ICLU when Levine's term of office was up in the spring. I seemed the most likely possibility because I had plenty of time to devote to the organization as well as organizational experience. Not having a law background, however, I felt inadequate for the job. I was finally persuaded to take it when these three promised to help me in every way possible. But before the election of officers took place I was stricken with violent intestinal cramps which had the doctors puzzled. I was in the hospital for a week under heavy sedation while they tried to figure out what was wrong with me. While I lay there suffering Levine barged into my room smoking a big, fat cigar and pleaded, "If you will just let me have the presidency one more year, then you can have it." I was in no condition to discuss the matter with him and said it was for the board to decide. I can still smell that cigar! My condition was finally diagnosed after the surgeon opened me up and found that I had a congenital condition which was easily rectified. When Don Murphy had news that my condition was not serious, he wrote me one of his pungent notes saying that this was an indication that the John Birch Society had not, as he thought, been able to put a curse on the ICLU. "Plainly Divine Justice might be at work on officers and leading lights," he said. He could see John Birch passing on orders to the Higher Command, "A stroke for Rockefeller . . . boils for Humphrey and gallstones for Louise Noun, etc." Apparently something had thwarted this disabolical plan and Murphy was delighted. Although Levine refused to withdraw his name as a candidate for ICLU president, there was no question that most of the board preferred me and I was duly elected.

A large part of my work as ICLU president was organizational; raising money, recruiting members, searching out people to head committees, organizing local chapters, and in general seeing that the organization ran as smoothly and effectively as possible. These were years of growth for the ICLU. Income increased from about $5,000 a year in 1965 to $20,694 in 1972 and membership more than doubled. In 1965 we rented office space in the Iowa Children's Home Society Building at Eleventh and Walnut and hired Oval Quist, a retired *Des Moines Register* editorial writer, as part-time executive secretary. Herb Kelly, also a retired editorial writer, took over the job when Quist retired in 1968. ICLU press releases written by these veteran journalists were always well written and since they usually went out under my name I became a pretty well-known public figure though not always a beloved one.

One of the major projects during my early years as ICLU president was a conference on civil liberties issues held in Des Moines in April 1966. Although I was vacationing with Maurie at the time of the conference, I helped with the planning. Among the subjects discussed were issues relating to religion and public education, such as schooling for Amish children, use of school buses for children attending parochial schools, shared time for religious education, and de facto segregation, as well as issues relating to due process of law, such as rights of the mentally ill and child custody. It is interesting to note that no issues relating to freedom of expression were discussed (perhaps we just took freedom of expression for granted), nor were any issues relating to feminist concerns on the program. My feminist consciousness was still so undeveloped that I never even thought of suggesting discussion of issues relating to women's rights. These did not become a matter of civil liberties concern until the arrival of the women's movement later in the decade. The conference was a success judging from the large attendance, but it was costly in terms of ICLU's limited finances. As Gil Cranberg remarked, it was an artistic success but a financial failure.

A big step ahead for the ICLU was when the organization became rich enough in 1966 to hire Dan Johnston at a small salary to serve as part-time legal counsel. Dan, who later handled the black armband case for the ICLU, was a tall, boyish-looking young lawyer who used to observe ICLU board meetings while he was still a student at Drake law school. He graduated the same year I became president of the ICLU and he immediately became active in civil liberties work. This was the beginning of a friendship which has continued to the present. Dan helped the ICLU establish an active litigation program. He recruited other lawyers for ICLU cases and he argued a number of them himself, including the black armband case.

Student unrest during the Vietnam War also kept the ICLU busy. Much rebellion was expressed in wearing long hair, which school authorities tried to repress by strict dress codes. In Colfax a girl was suspended from class for six weeks because she refused to conform to the rule "Hair must be kept one finger width above the eyebrows, clear across the forehead." In Washington, Iowa, the president of the student body was suspended for wearing his hair too long and the football coach ordered his players to keep away from this student. A high school girl in Decorah was suspended for defying the dress code by wearing slacks to a wrestling meet. In Maquoketa several students were suspended for long hair. The mother of one of these students sought help from the ICLU. She said she was the target of extensive hostility, receiving ugly phone calls and other harassment. A Maquoketa teacher who opposed the dress codes summed up public opinion with a perceptive statement: "Long hair equals drug addiction equals peaceniks equals communism." The ICLU took the position that a student's appearance with respect to dress and hair style should not be of concern to a school unless it actually disrupts the educational process or constitutes a threat to safety or health.

While ICLU lawyers challenged dress codes in court, I was involved with explaining the ICLU position to the public and in answering innumerable phone calls from students looking to the ICLU for information and help. I was particularly amused when I received

a call one evening from a young man who was being harassed because of his long hair. I thought his name sounded familiar and when
I asked if he were the son of William Scherle, a conservative member
of Congress from western Iowa, he said, "Yes, but don't tell my father
I contacted the ICLU." For an hour and a half one night I sat in my
apartment with the telephone receiver to my ear as the guest on a
call-in program of a Davenport radio station on the subject of dress
codes. Most callers were not interested in what I thought; they were
only anxious to express their own opinions, which seemed to be
largely related to what constitutes sexy dress. Several men thought
short skirts for girls made them too sexy, and one woman thought
boys aroused sexual feelings when their partially buttoned shirts ex-
posed too much of their chests. No one claimed that long hair for boys
was sexy but there was general agreement that dress codes were a
good idea. During the dress code furor I received a good deal of critical mail. For example, a person in Adel wrote, "Didn't you have guide
lines for your daughter that you didn't want some one else to enter
fere [sic] with? *Why don't you keep your mouth shut and vanish?*"
Like most such mail this note was unsigned. By 1970 judges in both
the Iowa northern and the southern districts of the Federal Court had
declared school dress codes unconstitutional and their decisions
marked the end of dress codes in most Iowa schools. By this time the
long-hair hysteria had abated and long hair was becoming stylish
even for members of the male establishment.

    The ICLU also defended student protesters at Grinnell College
who were charged in February 1969 with indecent exposure because
they removed their clothes at a meeting at the college addressed by a
representative of *Playboy Magazine.* Their action was in protest of
Playboy's treatment of women as "lapdog female playthings with ide-
alized proportions and their junior-executive-on-the-way-up posses-
sors." They called Playboy "prostitution on paper" and explained
that their purpose in disrobing was to "affirm the dignity of the
human body." Charges of indecent exposure were filed against these
students by Richard Turner, Iowa's flamboyant attorney general,
who saw political advantage in pursuing this case. Dan Johnston, the
ICLU attorney, represented the students at their trial in May 1969.
He claimed that there was nothing lewd or immoral about the students' actions and that to convict them was to deny them freedom of
expression. The judge, however instructed the jury that if it was
found that the students had disrobed in public, the jury had no
choice but to bring in a guilty verdict. Since the students had readily
admitted that they undressed, the jury reluctantly found them

guilty. In fact, the head of the jury was so indignant over the judge's instructions that he donated his pay as a juror to help with the students' appeals. The Iowa Supreme Court subsequently upheld the lower court's ruling and the United States Supreme Court refused to hear the case. Meanwhile, the Playboy Foundation sent the ICLU an unsolicited donation of $1,000 to help pay legal costs, which we gladly accepted. Subsequently, I received a letter from Kate Kasten, a recent Grinnell graduate and ardent feminist, protesting the acceptance of the gift from an organization which made its money exploiting women. Our reply was that since *Playboy* had in no way influenced the policies or proceedures of the ICLU, it was all right to take their money. Since that time my increased feminist consciousness leads me to think we should have refused the *Playboy* gift.

Meanwhile, my personal life changed in 1967 when I left my husband and had no more home responsibilities. Dan Johnston suggested that I go to law school. This idea appealed to me because of the desperate need for volunteer lawyers for civil liberties cases. Even at the age of fifty-nine I figured that after three years of school I could still have a number of years to practice law. My brother Joe, a lawyer, advised against my studying law. He predicted I would not like it. Ignoring Joe's warning, I entered Drake Law School in the fall of 1967 and lasted just one semester. The whole experience was traumatic. In the first place, I was the only woman (and a gray-haired one at that) in a class of some seventy young men fresh out of college. They acted as though I were a stranger in their midst and paid no attention to me. I didn't feel that I was in a position to force myself on them. Then there was the blatant sexism exhibited by Craig Sawyer, one of my professors, who looked over our class at its first meeting and said, "Excuse me, Louise, but there is always one woman to spoil every class." He then went on to define a woman as a household instrument that is meant to be screwed. At first I thought Sawyer was punishing me for his having been dropped from the black-armband case by the ICLU but on inquiry I found that this was a standard joke of his. One female law student even told me that she thought it was funny. I soon came to the realization that I was just too old to go back to school to master a field of learning in which I had no previous experience. I earned only average grades and I was not happy with my achievement. Furthermore, I found the whole experience physically exhausting. Getting to an eight o'clock class five days a week was traumatic and even carrying the heavy law textbooks was tiring! I didn't flunk out at the end of the semester, I just collapsed. Thus ended my aspiration to be a lawyer. I was happy to keep on being an

amateur in support of civil liberties. But this experience did make me
realize that if I wanted to work as a professional I should pursue a
field in which I already had some knowledge, which led me to apply
to the Art Center for a job.

In March 1968 I began a three-year term on the board of the
American Civil Liberties Union as a representative of the Iowa affili-
ate. This board met in New York several times a year. The ACLU,
from its founding during World War I to the late 1960s, had been gov-
erned by a small board of persons, most of whom lived in the New
York area. Not long after I became ICLU president, the ACLU board
was substantially enlarged in order to give its affiliates a greater voice
in ACLU affairs. When I joined the ACLU board there were fifty-six
members in all, only four of whom were women—Dorothy Kenyon,
Pauli Murray, Lois Forer, and I. Kenyon, a lawyer, was white, Anglo-
Saxon, and Protestant. She had grown up with all the advantages of
wealth and social position. At the age of eighty she was still vital,
witty, and committed to civil liberties and feminist causes. She had
served on the ACLU board since 1930. Murray, fifty-eight years old,
was a Negro (she preferred this term) orphaned at an early age and
brought up by an aunt in North Carolina. She overcame the disadvantages of poverty and of an inferior primary and secondary education in the South, to graduate from Hunter College in New York. She
studied law at Howard University and was turned down by Harvard
for postgraduate work in law because she was a woman. In 1968 she
was teaching at Brandeis University. She was an intense, courageous,
and dedicated worker for civil rights and women's rights. Lois Forer,
a lawyer who practiced in Philadelphia, felt shut out, as I did, by all
the men on the board. She soon chose not to continue as a board
member. Forer was subsequently appointed judge of the Court of
Common Pleas in Philadelphia.

To say that I was cowed by the vocal lawyers and the verbose aca-
demics who were the majority on the board is something of an un-
derstatement. For many months I was silent at board meetings,
knowing that sooner or later someone else would say what I wanted
to say but in a more articulate manner. But while I sat silent, I was
learning. I can't think of a better way to get an education on civil liberties issues than serving a term or two on the ACLU board. As the
women's movement emerged in the late 1960s, feminist issues increasingly came up for board consideration, the most important of
which was whether or not to endorse the Equal Rights Amendment.
By 1970 Kenyon was in poor health (she died of cancer in 1972) and
Murray became the chief spokesperson for women's issues on the

ACLU board. I didn't realize what this effort was costing her until she told me after one meeting how hard it was to carry this burden almost alone and asked me to back her up. I suddenly realized that here was an area where my voice was really needed.

The ACLU, along with most liberal organizations, had traditionally opposed an Equal Rights Amendment (ERA) as a threat to protective legislation for women. Until 1970 the ACLU took the position that lawsuits regarding women's rights should be tried on a case-by-case basis under the equal protection clause of the Fourteenth Amendment. Dorothy Kenyon supported this position wholeheartedly until 1970 when she became so frustrated over the Supreme Court's hesitancy in striking down legal differentiations based on sex that she enthusiastically joined the pro-ERA ranks. Although Pauli Murray thought that the ERA was the best guarantee of equality for women, she was willing to go along with the ACLU's position as long as she thought the ERA had only little chance of success.

I had first heard of the ERA when I joined the League of Women Voters in the 1940s and learned that one of the League's cardinal principles was opposition to it. I never questioned this position until I heard discussion of the pros and cons when the women's movement emerged in the late 1960s. I soon came to the conclusion that an ERA was needed because much so-called protective legislation actually worked against women's best interests, limiting the kinds of jobs they could hold and preventing them from working the hours of their choice. I have a distinct memory of a discussion of the ERA at an ACLU board meeting sometime prior to the ACLU's biennial convention in the spring of 1970. Kenyon and Murray both argued for the ACLU to support the ERA, while a labor leader from Michigan told how devastating it would be for women to lose laws designed to protect them. A motion to support the ERA received only three or four votes. Alan Rietman of the ACLU staff says he can find no record of this ERA discussion or vote but I can't believe that I dreamed it happened.

The ACLU position on women's rights changed radically in June 1970 at the organization's biennial conference, which met at New York University. This conference was made up of delegates from all the ACLU chapters throughout the country, a large proportion of whom were women who thought the ACLU should be more active in supporting women's rights. Because there were no women's rights issues on the conference program, Pauli Murray suggested forming a caucus to draw up a women's agenda for conference consideration. About twenty of us got together and drew up a comprehensive list of policies on sex discrimination and the conference voted to allow us to present these at a plenary session. Our program was adopted with hardly a word of debate, in contrast to the heated discussions which usually mark other ACLU policy decisions. This seeming indifference or condescension indicated to me that the conference did not take our program seriously. When I expressed my concern to Pauli Murray, she said, "Don't worry. They will." She was right. The ACLU board at its meeting in the fall of 1970 approved all the conference recommendations concerning women's rights, including support of the ERA, equal access to educational facilities, and reproductive freedom. A women's equality committee to monitor affirmative action within the ACLU was also appointed. I served on this committee until 1973 when I resigned because I was no longer an ACLU board member and thought others could be more effective. The following year I was elected to the Advisory Board of the ACLU, a purely honorary position that I still hold.

The women's rights agenda of the ACLU was the subject of a panel discussion and workshop at an ICLU conference held in Des Moines in April 1971. The fact that one of the three workshops at this meeting was devoted to women's rights sharply contrasted with the ICLU conference five years previously when the subject wasn't even mentioned. Despite this early lack of awareness, ICLU action in the area of women's rights actually began in 1967. At that time we supported an effort to liberalize Iowa's hundred-year-old abortion law which permitted abortions only to save the life of the mother. John Ely, a representative from Cedar Rapids and a devoted civil libertarian, managed to call a public hearing on a bill which he had introduced modifying Iowa's abortion law. A chaplain from Simpson College (I can't remember his name) and I met one evening to prepare a statement for the ICLU to present at the hearing. Since it seemed impossible to abolish the current law, we decided to ask only for modifications which would permit abortions in cases where the mental and physical health of the mother was threatened. When we finished writing our statement the chaplain asked which of us would represent the ICLU at the hearing. I said I was willing to do so but when the chaplain said he would like to make the presentation, I deferred to him. The chaplain then proceeded to comment that it was strange that women were so reluctant to speak up on the abortion issue. When I reminded him that I had just offered to speak at the hearing, he was very embarrassed and agreed that I should do so. There was a good deal of interest in the hearing and it drew a large crowd. Ely's bill, however, received only a couple of votes in committee and never reached the House for consideration. Two years later, a bill supported by Governor Ray which would have allowed abortions when the mental or physical health of the mother was threatened was defeated in the Senate. Meanwhile, a decision in California striking down a law similar to that in Iowa, gave us hope that we might nullify Iowa's abortion law through the courts. Before we could find a plaintiff, however, the Supreme Court of the United States ruled that no state can forbid an abortion in the first six months of pregnancy. The Iowa abortion law was subsequently declared unconstitutional.

Another feminist issue added to the agenda of the ICLU in the late 1960s concerned discrimination by public schools against pregnant girls and married students. Betty Turner, a Des Moines social worker, undertook the job of making a survey for the ICLU of how Iowa schools treated such students. We found that half of the school districts barred unmarried, expectant mothers from class at some stage of pregnancy. Twenty-five percent excluded married women who were pregnant, but did not necessarily bar their husbands. Some districts barred married students from attending high school at all, and about half denied them full participation in extracurricular activities such as athletics or school proms. The ICLU took the position that full educational opportunities should be provided for all high school students regardless of whether they were married, unmarried, or pregnant. Although a radical position at the time, this position is generally accepted by the public today. Meanwhile, schools, paying heed to court rulings barring discrimination against married and pregnant students, have dropped their discriminatory policies.

About the time my term as president of the ICLU ended in 1972, I was instrumental in forming an ICLU women's equality committee which I chaired for the next three years. Meanwhile, I had also become active in the Des Moines chapter of the National Organization for Women (NOW) which was organized during the summer of 1971. For the next several years a number of the feminist activities with which I was involved were sponsored jointly by the ICLU and NOW while others were sponsored only by one or the other of these organizations acting independently. During this period I pledged $15,000 over a period of three years to the ICLU Foundation to help pay the salary of a much-needed staff counsel with the stipulation that the foundation take at least one significant women's rights case each year. Gordon Allen, who was subsequently hired as counsel, did his best to fulfill this assignment. He was helpful in furthering the women's agenda although no landmark cases emerged. By the time my term on the ICLU board expired in 1975 I had come to the conclusion that, while the ICLU could be helpful in furthering women's legal rights, an organization such as NOW which was devoted solely to a broad range of women's social and economic issues offered me a more satisfactory way to pursue my feminist interests.

Rose Rosenfield pins a gold feather on her daughter. Louise headed a League of Women Voters "get out the vote" campaign for the first election in Des Moines under the council-manager plan. Each voter at the polls was given a gold feather.

Louise Noun and Kay Stroud, former presidents of the Des Moines League of Women Voters, in New York to receive a plaque citing the League for outstanding community service in 1949. The Des Moines organization was honored for its work in the campaign for council-manager government in the city, November 1950.

Louise, Maurie, and Susan—Sun Valley, Idaho, around 1953.

All-American Cities Jury, with George Gallup, chair, at the annual meeting of the National Municipal League, 1954.

Frank Miller cartoon inspired by Shirley
Chisholm's campaign for president of the
United States, 1972.

Shirley Chisholm

Claudia Morrisey, Mary Ann Campbell, Sally Hacker, and Louise Noun, in Sally Hacker's apartment, around 1973.

Sally Hacker after her move to Oregon.

Louise Noun, January 1970. (Joan Liffring-Zug photo)

Louise Noun honoring pioneer Iowa suffragist Annie Savery on August 26, 1972, the anniversary of the ratification of the Nineteenth Amendment. This portrait is in the Iowa Historical Museum's collection. (Des Moines Register photo)

Jason Flora, Louise Noun, and Susan Noun Flora, 1975. (Marjorie Nichols Hufnagel photo)

Isabel Bishop, American (1902–1988). Women
Walking in the Subway Station, #2, *1963.*
Etching/aquatint, 9½″ ×10¼″.

Louise Bourgeois, American (b. 1904). Figure Voile, c. 1949. Ink on paper, 9¾″ × 12¾″.

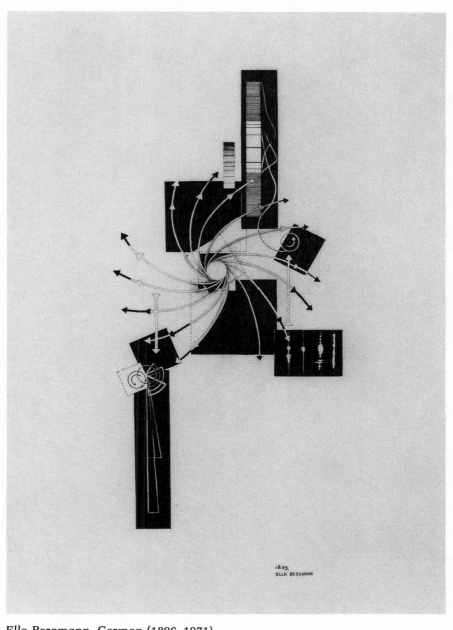

Ella Bergmann, German (1896–1971).
OB 193, c. 1924. Pencil and ink on paper,
22½″ × 17¾″.

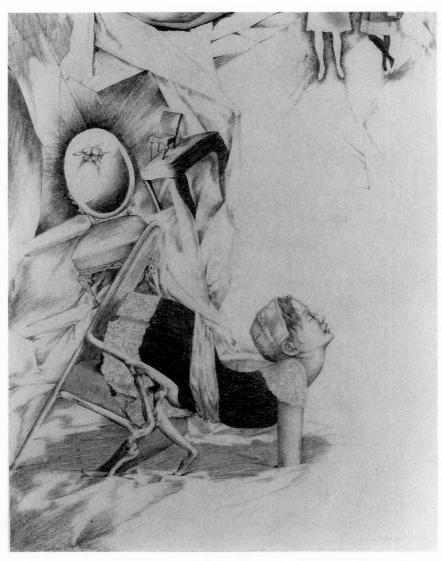

Dorothea Tanning, American (b. 1910).
Musical Chairs, 1949. Pencil on paper, 24½″
× 19¼″.

Hannah Höch, German (1895–1978). Der Weg
(The Path), 1927. Oil, 27″ × 25″.

*Natalia Gontcharova, Russian (1881–1962).
Fishers, 1909. Oil on canvas, 46″ × 40″.*

8

FEMINISM

Occasionally someone asks me why I am a feminist. My reply is that I am a feminist because I am a woman. Although this is a somewhat flippant response, it is basically true. As children, my sister and I were subject to Mother's tongue-lashings while my brother could do no wrong. As young adults my brother was offered a monetary reward for not smoking while my sister and I were offered only our parents' disapproval. As a graduate student, I was told to go home and get married when I asked the school for help in getting a job. As a wife I was expected to take my husband's name and devote myself to his welfare. As a woman I couldn't belong to the Des Moines Foreign Policy Association where some of the brightest men of the community met to discuss foreign affairs. As a woman I was ineligible for membership on the board of the Des Moines Art Center, and when the bar against women was lifted, I could not expect to aspire to any position of leadership because I was a woman. As a woman of means who would have been criticized if I had looked for a paid position, I was expected to serve my community as a volunteer in jobs which were often intellectually stultifying and unappreciated.

Perhaps I would not have been so ready to become an active feminist if I hadn't had the example of my mother, whom I now see as a frustrated feminist who resented the societal restraints she met because she was a woman. Mother took part in the fight for women's suffrage, financially helped other women to get educated, and worked for the recognition of women's contributions to the community. In becoming an active feminist I was, in a sense, helping to fulfill my mother's dream of making women full partners in our society. Yet during Mother's lifetime I never had much sympathy for or understanding of her feminist concerns. I always took Mother's support of women's suffrage for granted and I assumed that anyone with a modicum of common sense would want women to vote. The pantsuit she wore for gardening seemed a little odd but I never viewed it as an expression of feminism and I couldn't understand why she would campaign to secure the community award for a woman she didn't even know. In fact, as her daughter, I felt Mother was much more a person to be feared than to be emulated. Yet in my old age I am sometimes taken aback by how much I seem like her. This was first brought home to me a number of years ago by my sister. I was scolding her for making fun of Rose Koeger, the maid who worked for Mother for so many years. Ruth burst into tears and said, "You say you hate Mother, and yet you sound just like her." Time and maturity have helped me dissolve a lot of that hate, and I can now say with some degree of pride that in many ways I am a good deal like my mother. I only hope that I am less feared and more loved than she was.

Despite my resentment of the many restraints I felt because I am a woman, I never looked at these restraints from a feminist point of view until the current women's movement. In fact, when I was told by my professor in graduate school to just go home and get married, I felt a sense of personal shame and defeat. I never told anyone about this advice until the feminist movement came along and I could view it not as a personal put-down, but as a prime example of male chauvinism. It was only when I made this connection that I could be relieved of my feeling of shame and guilt and express my long-suppressed anger. Although I was well aware of and resented the unjust treatment I experienced because of my sex, I accepted it as a given in our society. I might not like it but there was nothing I could do about it. After all, who ever said life was fair?

The turning point in my attitude came during the period when I was getting psychiatric help. When I started treatment I was a person in despair, trapped in an unsatisfactory marriage. Furthermore, I was a person with no sense of self-worth, who even viewed my successes as failures. I can remember telling Sidney Sands that I was disturbed about the successful finance drive I had headed for the League of Women Voters. I complained that it had been too successful. Sidney asked why it had been too successful. I couldn't tell him except that perhaps too much would be expected of me in the future. It took a long while to develop a sense of self-esteem but eventually I was able to face situations in my life—both good and bad—without my sense of self-worth being threatened. I also came to realize that I was not necessarily trapped in my marriage and that I had the choice of staying or leaving. I finally chose the latter alternative. My divorce came almost simultaneously with the arrival of the women's movement but it was not the women's movement that gave me the courage to leave my husband. It was because I had enough self-confidence to brave societal condemnation and strike out on my own. Nonetheless, being part of the women's movement was like finding a congenial home where as a woman I could find sympathetic company and where we women could support each other by joining together in fighting our oppression.

My interest in feminism began in 1959 when I agreed to be the featured speaker at women's day at the University of Northern Iowa. As a topic for this talk I decided that I would investigate the history of the woman suffrage movement in Iowa. I knew that Amelia Bloomer, a suffragist known for the type of reform dress that bears her name, and Carrie Chapman Catt, who led the woman suffrage forces to victory in 1920, both were Iowa women so I decided to base my talk on their achievements. Unfortunately, I came down with bronchitis which prevented me from giving the talk. This canceled talk, however, marked the beginning of my interest in the history of the woman suffrage movement in Iowa. I was astonished to learn that there had been a fifty-year struggle to obtain the vote in Iowa and that there were many women prior to my mother's time who had also worked for the cause. Thus began a research and writing project which occupied much of my time for the next ten years and resulted in the publication in 1969 of my book, *Strong-minded Women: The Emergence of the Woman-Suffrage Movement in Iowa.*

In researching the history of the struggle for woman suffrage I used to wonder if I would have been on the liberal or conservative side of the suffrage movement in the nineteenth century. Would I have sided with Lucy Stone and other moderate Bostonians, who tried to avoid extreme actions that might antagonize the public, or would I have sided with the New York branch of the movement headed by Susan B. Anthony and Elizabeth Cady Stanton, who dismayed the Bostonians by discussing such taboo subjects as divorce and birth control? (The Bostonians called these "side issues.") I hoped I would have sided with Anthony and Cady Stanton. On the Iowa scene, would I have supported the brilliant and articulate Annie Savery of Des Moines, wife of the owner of the Savery Hotel, who made a speech at the 1871 convention of the Iowa Woman Suffrage

Association defending the right of free-love advocate Victoria
Woodhull to a place in the suffrage ranks? As a result of Savery's defense of Woodhull's right to associate with suffragists, she was
branded a "free lover" and ostracized by other suffragists. In the
spring of 1872 Savery was publicly humiliated by the Iowa Senate
when it voted against allowing her to deliver a prearranged address
on woman suffrage. The senators had been asked by the Polk County
Woman Suffrage Association to deny Savery permission to speak because this organization did not want to be represented by anyone
even remotely associated with free love. (The senators were only too
willing to comply.) I was indignant at the treatment Savery received.
Certainly I would have been on her side.

    While I was writing my book it never occurred to me that the
women's movement was anything but a matter of history or that I
would soon have an opportunity to make similar choices in the wake
of a new wave of feminism. During the 1960s I was aware that there
was a renewed interest in women's issues. I sent for the 1963 report of
President Kennedy's Commission on the Status of Women and in
February 1965 I attended a conference sponsored by the Governor's
Commission on the Status of Women (a nonfunded body appointed
by Gov. Harold Hughes in 1963). Co-sponsors of this conference included the YWCA, AAUW, and nine professional businesswomen's
groups. I had never been associated with any of these organizations
so I felt somewhat like an outsider at this meeting. The conference
covered a wide range of issues relating to the problems of women in
the labor force, issues which I had never had to face personally. I suddenly realized how narrow my point of view was—I had always
thought of women's issues in terms of voting rights and equal rights
to property and child custody, rather than in terms of rights relating
to the needs of women employed outside the home. This conference
marked just one more step in my education as a feminist. Although I
am not a hoarder of ephemeral literature, I still have the 1964 report
of the Governor's Commission on the Status of Women which was
distributed at this meeting.

    My education as a feminist was also broadened in 1964 when I
acquired a copy of the spring issue of Daedalus, the journal of the
American Academy of Arts and Sciences, titled "The Woman in
America." I was particularly impressed with Alice Rossi's essay on
"Equality Between the Sexes." Rossi pointed out that law alone cannot achieve equality for women. She emphasized that there needs to
be a change in social attitudes and institutions before women can be
accepted as equals in our society. I recently reread this article and

was impressed that Rossi, as late as 1964, could comment that there was hardly a feminist spark left among American women. As far as I was concerned, feminism at that time was purely a matter of theoretical interest, probably because there was as yet no feminist movement to encourage me to action.

Betty Friedan's *Feminine Mystique*, published in 1963, did not impress me as a significant book. During my research on the history of woman suffrage, I had come across many books by women who found an outlet for their discontents in writing about their oppression and I considered Friedan's book just another one of this genre. I thoroughly agreed with everything Friedan had to say, but in retrospect, I think the reason I was unimpressed was that Friedan suggested no ways for women to improve their status as second-class citizens. What I failed to realize was that in describing women's discontent and creating a name for it, Friedan was helping fan the feminist spark into a full-blown fire. Helping feed the fire was a small group of women, including Friedan, who founded the National Organization for Women in 1965. A few years later Friedan spoke at Drake University in an effort to spark interest in NOW among Drake students. I went to hear Friedan but found her to be a poor speaker and not a person to move women to action. My impression, however, was not shared by thirty-one-year-old Virginia Watkins of Des Moines, who was impressed enough by Friedan's book and by hearing her speak to take the lead in organizing a local chapter of NOW.

My recollection is that I jumped at the opportunity to help organize a Des Moines chapter of NOW but Virginia tells me that when she asked me to help her recruit ten feminists, the minimum number required to convene a chapter, I told her that I was sympathetic but that I thought this a job for younger women. Although I didn't recruit members for Des Moines NOW, I was a charter member, attending my first meeting at Virginia's home in the late winter or spring of 1971. Virginia recalls that Dannie Rosenfield, my brother's wife, and I were regular attenders of NOW meetings during the early days and that one or the other of us would put a little cash in the till at each meeting to help publicize the group. At this time activities of the group included work to insure maternity leave for teachers in the West Des Moines school system, efforts to add sex discrimination as the responsibility of the Des Moines Human Rights Commission, and writing letters to members of Congress in support of the ERA, which had not yet been approved by this body. While I was supportive of these efforts most of my feminist activities at this time were still under the umbrella of the ICLU where I chaired the women's equality committee. I soon came to realize, however, that working within a legal framework was not enough. In order to change the status of women in our society, it was necessary to change basic social attitudes and NOW offered a means to help accomplish this task. As I became more active in NOW I gradually withdrew from ICLU activities. Virginia Watkins served as the first president of the Des Moines NOW but she moved to Minneapolis in the fall of 1971. She was succeeded by Kay Plymat, a nurse, who served as president for two years. Irene Talbott (Tally), who worked for the Iowa Commission for the Blind, took over the presidency in January 1973—at the same time that I joined the Des Moines NOW board as a member at large. By the time Tally's term of office was up in 1974, I was deep into NOW activities and willing to assume the presidency for the next two years.

During the early days of NOW we were a small, impecunious group with a lot of energy and enthusiasm but without an office. The Friends Service Committee subsequently generously agreed to let us use their number for a phone listing and to take our calls. When NOW decided to run a classified ad in the *Des Moines Register* asking interested women to call for information about our organization, the Service Committee started getting some very strange calls from men. We found that the "Personal" heading under which the ad had been run also carried ads for massage parlors. It apparently was worded so that there was confusion about our message. We hastily pulled the ad. Later, when NOW developed several video advertisements for use as public service spots by television stations, I was surprised to find that the spots carried my telephone number for those seeking further information. A few interested women did respond to these ads, but there were also obscene and crank calls from males. I didn't complain for it was all for the good of the cause. It seemed to me, however, that these spots continued to be run endlessly.

It is difficult to convey the feeling of excitement which surrounded feminists in the 1970s. We were united in combating our oppression as women, full of energy for our mission, and happily unaware of the backlash that would hamper achieving our objectives. Much of the early work was in the form of consciousness-raising; small groups of women meeting regularly to share personal experiences, problems, and feelings. From this sharing women increased their awareness and understanding of feminism. They learned that what they thought were purely personal problems had social causes that could be attacked through political action. I never participated in a consciousness-raising group as I felt my feminist consciousness was already sufficiently developed. Other activities included handing out information on the legal rights of married women at bridal fairs and picketing beauty contests. I was amused when a representative of the Junior Jaycees contacted me in the fall of 1976 to invite me to be a judge at a "Des Moines Junior Miss Pageant" which his organization was sponsoring. The "pageant" (i.e., beauty contest) was to be held on the Drake University campus and the winner was to receive a substantial scholarship. The man who called me was completely taken aback when I attacked the concept of beauty contests and told him that I could never lend my support to a project which judged women by the shape of their bodies rather than by their merits as scholars. Subsequent to this call I alerted Drake women and we arranged to picket the contest. Another NOW activity was presenting to selected businessmen the "Barefoot and Pregnant Award" for their chauvinist treatment of female employees. I was too self-conscious a member of the "establishment" to take part in these ventures although I was amused at the discomfort of the men who received them. In 1974 Sally Hacker, a Des Moines NOW member who taught sociology at Drake, led a group of women who put a "witch's hex" on the new seven-million-dollar stadium then under construction at Iowa State University. The objective of the hex was to cause the stadium to fall to the ground since the money to build it had been stolen from (i.e., could better have been spent for) child care. Coincidentally, part of the stadium did collapse six months later, probably because it was built on a flood plain. The women happily put out a press release accepting responsibility and warning of other dire consequences to come if child care wasn't funded. Another feminist activity of the early 1970s was the organization of women's health groups which explored ways for women to take greater control over their own bodies.

My main contribution at this time was along more conventional lines. I helped organize a women's employment conference sponsored jointly by NOW and the ICLU in early December 1971. We drew an overflow crowd of women who were unhappy with their low wages and their lack of opportunity for advancement because of sex discrimination in the workplace. Roxanne Conlin, assistant attorney general, told these women that discrimination because of sex was now against the law and explained how they could file charges against discriminating employers. I had the feeling that these women needed a quick fix for their complaints and that we were offering them only the prospect of a long, drawn-out legal form of redress, which might or might not be successful. Unfortunately most women, then and now, are fearful of filing complaints for fear of losing their jobs and of being blacklisted when seeking other employment.

NOW brought me into contact with a group of dynamic feminists, a number of whom were to become close friends. Outstanding among these women was Sally Hacker, a beautiful, soft-spoken, radical woman who wore boots and rode a motorcycle to school. Sally was thrown out of high school in the eleventh grade because she was pregnant. She married the father of her child and moved to Chicago where she graduated from a community college. She then won a scholarship to the University of Chicago where she eventually received her Ph.D. degree. Sally described herself as a radical feminist anarchist who believed in working for a cooperative social order. She and several other Des Moines feminists rented a house on Motley Street which they named Motley House. This house, which they ran as a cooperative venture, was not far from where I live. It was a place where I could go for feminist conversation and where feminist actions were likely to be hatched. The Motley cooperative broke up after a year and the members scattered to other locations in the city. I missed this meeting place.

Sally Hacker did more than anyone in the movement to broaden my feminist perspective. I remember going with her to visit with a very tough, strong, low-income woman who was having difficulties in her job at the telephone company because she had taken time off to care for a sick child. Her supervisor had suggested that her husband could assume some of her child-care responsibilities. This woman commented that this was impossible as her husband earned twice as much as she and that they couldn't afford to have him take time off from work. She also told us of the pressure under which the employees in her department worked. The experience gave me an insight into the lives of employees of the telephone company that I could have gotten in no other way. Sally also introduced me to the radical community in Des Moines, a group of very serious young men and women who were convinced that some form of socialism or anarchism was the best solution to the world's ills. I accepted an invitation to take part in an "educational"—a two-day session of lectures and discussion—sponsored by these people, and I did a vast amount of background reading in preparation for this event. All this broadened my understanding of how socialists viewed the capitalist system, but I could not see how their utopian hopes could come to fruition. In addition, my personal well-being was too much dependent on the capitalist system to have any desire to discard it.

After Sally left Des Moines in 1975 I would get notes from her suggesting that I meet her at various feminist or sociological meetings. I attended two annual conventions of the Women's Studies Association with her and now regret that I didn't join her at various European conferences that she thought I would enjoy. Through Sally I kept track of what was going on in the more radical wing of the women's movement. At the Women's Study Conference in Columbus, Ohio, I went with her to hear a discussion on pornography led by feminists who were opposed to its suppression because they, themselves, found it stimulating. Sally thought these women might cause a serious split in the feminist movement, but as a matter of fact the most serious split has come between those who oppose pornography and want it censored and those, like myself, who also oppose pornography but are against its censorship (except in cases involving children) on First Amendment grounds. On this issue I find myself in disagreement with a number of Des Moines NOW members.

Sally headed the national American Telephone and Telegraph task force of NOW, which worked with the federal Equal Employment Opportunity Commission, helping to substantiate the commission's charges of systematic discrimination by the telephone company against minorities and women. These groups were generally confined to the lowest-paying positions and denied opportunities for advancement. This was a very important case not only because AT&T was the largest employer of women in the United States but also because it was the first case of its kind to come before the courts. The case was finally settled in January 1973 when the company agreed to pay $38 million in back pay and wage increases. This amount fell far short of the $3.5 billion in back pay due since discrimination became illegal. Nonetheless, the AT&T case was important because it set a precedent for other EEOC legal actions. I tried to understand Sally's explanations of the AT&T action but much of it was too technical for my comprehension. Sally was particularly interested in the effects of technology on women's employment and noted that as women in the telephone system began to be promoted to higher ranks, the promotions were often to jobs that would soon be abolished because of automation.

In 1975 when Sally received a fellowship to do research at the Massachusetts Institute of Technology she left Des Moines. She later became professor of sociology at Oregon State University in Corvalis. Sally's activities in general were apparently so threatening to Drake that for years after her departure the administration tried to screen out radical female applicants for faculty positions by asking if they rode a motorcycle! A heavy smoker, Sally died of lung cancer in August 1988 at the age of fifty-one. At the time of her death she had just completed a study of gender and technology in the Mondragon Cooperative of the Basque area of Spain.

When I learned that NOW was holding a national convention in Los Angeles in September 1971, I decided to attend although I was just becoming active in NOW activities. This seemed to be a good way to learn about what was going on nationally. When I got there I found there was a lot of turmoil because lesbians were asking for NOW's support in seeking elimination of discrimination against them. This was a touchy issue which Aileen Hernandez, NOW president, tried to avoid by calling it a "side issue" which should not deflect NOW from its avowed purpose of eliminating discrimination against women generally. I was struck by the similarity of Hernandez's argument to those of the conservative feminists a century earlier who called issues relating to marriage and divorce "side issues." Personally I was not yet entirely comfortable in dealing with lesbian issues and I had to be convinced that they belonged under the feminist umbrella. At this time I neither knew lesbians who openly admitted their sexual orientation nor had I fully considered the ramifications of their oppression. Yet I knew from my study of women's history that what seems like a radical position today often turns out to be accepted as mainstream later on. So I was willing to support a relatively innocuous resolution adopted by the convention which declared, "A woman's right to her own person includes the right to define and express her own sexuality and to choose her own lifestyle; therefore we acknowledge the oppression of lesbians as a legitimate concern of feminism."

I was particularly excited about the resolution the convention adopted on volunteerism, condemning volunteer labor for social services. This kind of activity, the NOW resolution pointed out, is an extension of woman's traditional role of nurturer. It provides a mystique for the exploitation of women, prevents them from earning money, and keeps them in a powerless position. Because such work is unpaid in a society which equates status with wealth, it reinforces women's low self-image. Furthermore, the volunteer system removes jobs from the paid labor market that would otherwise be available to women. NOW did support change-oriented volunteerism directed at achieving the basic rights of all persons to equal opportunity and economic security, but did not support service-oriented volunteerism that deals with symptoms of poverty and not its causes.

For me, this discussion of volunteerism provided the "click" of understanding by which I suddenly realized that a lot of my frustrations over the years were due to time I had spent doing volunteer work. Selling rummage and driving children to clinics did nothing to enhance my self-image. These jobs should have been paid positions for women who truly needed the work. It also helped to explain my unsatisfactory relationship with the Art Center where my status as a volunteer deprived me of the respect I might have had if I had held a paid position. I brought the message on volunteerism back to the Des Moines NOW and we subsequently formed a task force on volunteerism whose goal was to raise consciousness about the implications of women's free labor. Many women were threatened by our questioning of their traditional roles as volunteers. It was difficult to make people understand that free labor for social change was all right, but not free labor to maintain the status quo. After hearing me discuss volunteerism on television, one woman in western Iowa told my friend, John Chrystal, that I had just taken away the whole meaning of her life. The Waterloo Junior League proved to be an unfriendly audience despite the fact that they had invited me to speak on volunteerism. This was understandable since service volunteerism has traditionally been the heart of Junior League philosophy. One member came up to me after my speech and said the Waterloo League should have listened to the Des Moines League, which had advised against asking me to speak. Despite our critics, I think our task force did a great deal toward making women evaluate the kinds of volunteer jobs that they undertake. Now that so many women are in the work force, the issue of volunteerism is not as relevant as it was fifteen or twenty years ago, although much of the work of charitable organizations is still dependent on free female labor.

During the summer of 1973 I decided to investigate United Way funding of recreational agencies serving boys and girls. It was common knowledge that the Boy Scouts were better funded than the Girl Scouts or the Campfire Girls and I thought it would be worthwhile to find out exactly what the differences in funding were for all the recreational agencies serving the youth of Des Moines. If the discrepancies in funding were as large as I thought they might be, my research could be the basis for feminist action. The United Way office was willing to tell me how much the United Way allotted to each recreational agency, but they refused to tell me what the total budgets of these agencies were. They said I would have to go to the agencies themselves to obtain this information. Thus what I had originally thought would be a simple job turned out to be a time-consuming one. As long as I had to go to the individual agencies, I decided to collect more information than simply the amount of their total budgets, so I also asked about salary scales, number of youth served, and program activities. I found that the Girl Scouts and the Campfire Girls combined served more than twice as many persons as the Boy Scouts and at about half the cost. The budget of the YMCA was more than twice that of the YWCA. Professional salaries for the agencies serving girls were much lower than the salaries paid by agencies serving boys. When I had gathered this information I thought it would be courteous to visit with United Way director, Robert Mabie, about the results of my study. Although I made an appointment to see him at a mutually agreed upon time, he was not in his office when I arrived. I was left sitting for an hour, waiting in vain for him to show up. I was furious. So while I waited I enlarged the scope of my study by leaving Mabie a list of questions about the number of women and minorities on his staff. When I got no response during the following week, I called Mabie and let him know how very angry I was. He then made an appointment to see me at my apartment to discuss the information I had asked for. He offered no excuse for not showing up for our original appointment other than to say he had "goofed," nor did he give me any meaningful figures about his staff. He did give me a copy of the United Way affirmative action policy but said he had been too busy hiring staff to pay any attention to affirmative action! Later, the president of the United Way board gave me, sub-rosa, a list of United Way employees and their salaries which showed that no professional woman on the staff was earning as much as any of the professional men.

After I had collected this information I wasn't sure how to proceed so I brought up the subject of the United Way at a NOW meeting and asked for suggestions. I found that the women at this meeting not only resented the United Way because of unfair distribution of funds, but also because of strong-arm collection methods used in workplace solicitation. They felt undue pressure to contribute in order to protect their jobs. As a result, there was a good deal of interest in what I had done and a NOW United Way task force was formed. Working with this task force was a memorable experience for me. The individual research project which I had started had turned into a true group experience with every member participating in research and evaluation and all decisions being made by consensus. Usually my personal inclination is to work alone but the United Way task force showed me how a group working together can enlarge one's viewpoint and provide for more effective action.

In order to give the task-force members a better understanding of the information I had collected, we decided to revisit all the agencies that I had previously interviewed. In addition, we made an effort to determine how many low-income youth were served by these agencies. We found that all of them, with the exception of the Boys' Club, which excluded girls from its program, were serving primarily middle-class persons. Since the majority of the poor in our society are women, it was obvious that the United Way was not serving the people who were most in need of services.

Because we were hearing many complaints about compulsory giving, we decided to investigate the methods used to persuade (or coerce) wage earners to be contributors. We found that, generally, solicitation was done by office supervisors, and employees under their supervision were fearful that they would be penalized in their jobs if they did not give. At Northwestern Bell it was well known that people who failed to give a predetermined "fair share" of their pay to the United Way were not promoted. At Blue Cross/Blue Shield "contributing" to the United Way was a condition of employment. Furthermore, we found that the United Way "Fair Share" guideline for giving was grossly unfair. Workers earning $4,500—a figure below the poverty level for a family of four—were asked to give $27 a year and those earning as little as $2,500 were asked to give $15 a year. This meant that the poverty-stricken and the working poor, a majority of whom were female, were being pressured to contribute to a fund that returns money and services to a largely white, middle-class clientele. Company executives, on the other hand, were expected to give proportionately much less than their lowest-paid employees. The director of Blue Cross/Blue Shield told us he thought this was fair because as a high-salaried man he owned two homes and needed more money to cover his living expenses.

Our task force report was in the form of an open letter to the United Way that we released in the spring of 1974. We recommended that in order to make recreational programs equitable, they should no longer be divided by sex; that greater effort should be made to make services of recreational agencies available to low-income persons; and that instead of a volunteer bureau, the United Way should establish a bureau to help create and find paying jobs for low-income persons. We also recommended that solicitation be directed at corporate and business profits rather than at salaries of employees, and that employee contributions be truly voluntary. We criticized the United Way for its refusal to release figures that would reveal corporate contributions as distinct from those of their employees.

When I delivered our report to the *Des Moines Register* I felt somewhat like a traitor to a sacred institution. In the past I had been a part of the system, soliciting door-to-door for contributions to the United Way. My mother and my brother (probably also my sister) had all headed United Way drives and it was always taken for granted in our family that the United Way should be supported. I was reassured when Drake Mabry, the city editor, didn't seem shocked at the material I gave him. He said I was not alone in complaining about the United Way. The media, including the *Des Moines Register,* gave our report wide publicity and I was interviewed for the evening television news while standing in front of a new YMCA wing containing handball courts. I enjoyed pointing out that these expensive new courts would primarily serve businessmen of the community while the needs of low-income people were being neglected. During the fall United Way campaign I joined other NOW members in standing on the sidewalks of downtown Des Moines and handing out leaflets questioning United Way tactics. This was my first experience with carrying a message to the streets. I was very self-conscious and had an impulse to hide when I saw someone I knew coming along. When Dannie Rosenfield, my close friend and sister-in-law, was asked that day if I were leafleting with other NOW members, she replied, "Louise would never do anything like that." I not only did it, but in the end, I overcame my self-consciousness and got satisfaction out of having developed the courage to confront an establishment institution.

A few weeks after we issued our United Way report, the United Way board of directors agreed to meet with our task force in an open session. At this meeting we sat around a large U-shaped table with representatives of the media standing in the background. We were allowed a limited amount of time to present our views but we found little favorable response from United Way board members. We were promised that the United Way would be more cooperative in giving us the kinds of information we had been requesting, but in fact none was forthcoming. The United Way also admitted the validity of our complaint about expecting persons earning wages below the poverty level to be contributors and agreed to stop this practice. They did this for a few years but then went back to their same old ways.

Six months after our meeting with the United Way board, we issued a second open letter saying that we could see few indications that the United Way was making good-faith efforts to meet our criticisms. We cited continued pressure on low-income employees to give to the United Way and we listed specific complaints we had received.

These can be summed up by a clerk at the Valley National Bank who called me to complain, "If you don't give, your name is mud." (This woman was so fearful about her job that she didn't even tell me her name.) Our letter also deplored the continued secrecy concerning levels of giving to the United Way. "We have more than a hunch," we said, "that the United Way operates as a Robin Hood in reverse— serving an essentially white, middle-class and, in many instances, male public from the energies and contributions of lower-income folks and middle-class women volunteers." Without basic data, we said, we had no way of proving our assumption.

Our United Way action got national attention and we heard from people in all parts of the country asking for copies of our study. I prepared a "how to" sheet for other groups who wanted to embark on a similar action. It is hard to know what the impact of our action was but certainly the women's movement can take credit for some changes in United Way operations. Since 1974 women for the first time have chaired the board of the United Way. The current director is a woman. The Boys' Club now admits girls, women may use YMCA facilities, and YWCA facilities are open to men. But there are still many inequities. The Boy Scouts per capita still get the lion's share of the funds given to scouting activities, and low-paid employees, even those earning below the poverty level, continue to be pressured to give disproportionate amounts of their wages to the United Way. In addition, the United Way now offers a phoney, donor-option plan by which contributors are told they can specify a particular United Way agency to receive their contributions. In fact, donor funds going to such agencies are deducted from other funds these agencies get from the United Way. When I learned about this situation from stories in the *Des Moines Register,* I was inspired to call my old friend, Betty Turner, who also questioned United Way methods, and together we wrote an article published on the editorial page of the *Des Moines Register* on October 21, 1988, in which we called attention to the NOW report of fourteen years ago and commented that their solicitation methods had not changed since that time.

The most tangible evidence of my activity as a feminist is the Young Women's Resource Center in Des Moines. This was founded in 1976 by a group of women active in the women's justice program of the Friends Service Committee and the NOW task force on juvenile justice. One of the concerns of the NOW task force was the plight of girls who were often sent to reform school because of sexual promiscuity though they were breaking no laws. We wanted to do away with this unfair practice and also find a positive way to help young women

avoid involvement with the juvenile justice system. At this time
there was a good deal of government money available for juvenile
justice programs and various organizations were looking for ways to
spend it. Among them was the Drake University psychology department, which developed a proposal for a residential home for girls
under the jurisdiction of the juvenile court, to be called Achievement Place. Treatment would be by behavior modification and residents were to be given points for positive behavior such as smiling
and brushing their teeth. This kind of treatment was antithetical to
the feminist philosophy of autonomy for girls and women. The Drake
psychology department at that time was dominated by behaviorists
and it was obvious that they were searching for guinea pigs for their
theories. In the spring of 1975 Drake invited representatives of NOW,
the Friends Service Committee, the ICLU, and other groups to a
luncheon to hear about this project and to enlist support for a grant
application for government funding. Unfortunately for Drake, they
invited the wrong people. One by one we got up and attacked the
concept of the project. Sally Hacker, who had come with a group of
her students, said she didn't believe that such a structured situation
was advantageous for young women. Gordon Allen, attorney for the
ICLU, pointed out that a third of the proposed budget was earmarked
for videotapes and related equipment to be used by the psychology
department for their own purposes. Our complaints seemed to have
been effective because Achievement Place was not funded.

After opposing the proposal for Achievement Place, Des Moines
feminists felt obligated to search seriously for an alternative, non-
coercive facility. Our aim was to meet the needs of young women in a
facility that would operate in accordance with feminist philosophy.
We began to meet on a more or less regular basis—usually in my living room—to hold wide-ranging discussions about how best to
achieve our goals. At first we thought in terms of a group home for
girls with a minimum of rules and where the residents could come
and go as they pleased. Attractive as this idea was, we soon realized
that there was no possibility of getting funding for such an unstruc-
tured project. So we gave up the idea of a residential facility and decided to develop some kind of a drop-in center for young women.
This idea developed into the concept of a Young Women's Resource
Center which would offer free counseling, job training, and other resources for helping young women solve their problems and become
self-reliant individuals. Meanwhile, we investigated projects in
other communities but could find none that were close to what we
had in mind. We also consulted with a variety of social workers and

others to get their ideas of how to proceed. I shall never forget one of these "others" with whom we visited, a young woman whom a friend brought to our meeting one night. She told us of her life—raped by her stepfather as a child, beaten by her mother when she told on him, running away and sleeping under cars or with men she picked up in order to get a warm night's sleep. She now had a nine-to-five job and was determined to stay off the streets. Her advice was to have food in the refrigerator for hungry clients. This was my first (and only) close-up view of a street kid.

We incorporated the Young Women's Resource Center in the fall of 1975 and the following months were spent enlarging the board and seeking funding. The first (and only) male to join our board prior to the opening of the center had trouble understanding what feminism was all about and soon resigned. I recall the consternation he caused when he suggested that we could measure success by the number of clients who didn't get pregnant. I had hoped that we could recruit someone with ability to head the board but our first two presidents proved to be ineffective leaders so I agreed to take the job. Since I was the only person on the board with connections to likely donors, I also undertook the responsibility for fund-raising. Rather than going to corporations first, I went to wealthy women in the community and asked them for substantial contributions. This was a successful tactic and gave us a sound basis for asking for funding from businessmen and local foundations. By the end of 1977 funding for the first year seemed assured and we went ahead with locating space and hiring a director. The Center was opened in early January 1978.

The Young Women's Resource Center, now over ten years old, has made a permanent place for itself in the community. It offers a variety of programs for young women ranging from individual counseling to group activities for teenage mothers. The Center has also developed an in-school program where staff members of the resource center are invited to discuss issues relating to sex with mixed classes of girls and boys. I chose to leave the board permanently in 1982 as I felt I had served long enough. However, by 1985 the board had become so conservative that it voted to rescind its personnel policy of nondiscrimination because of sexual orientation. I found out at this time how emotionally involved I still was with this group. Their action seemed pure treason in light of the liberal standards of the center's founders and I went to a board meeting and expressed my anger in no uncertain terms. About a year later the board saw the error of its ways and reinstituted its nondiscrimination policy. Subsequent changes in board membership have brought board philosophy back to a more liberal stance. I am proud of my part in establishing the Young Women's Resource Center and I hope as the years go by it will not stray too far from the ideals of its feminist mothers.

While the Young Women's Resource Center has proved to be a success story, the Iowa Women's Law Center that I sponsored never got off the ground. This center was proposed by Barb Yates, a tall, athletic, brilliant, radical feminist, who had graduated from the University of Iowa Law School in 1975 and was looking for a socially useful job. Barb had the idea of educating women in the mysteries of the law, both to provide women with a self-help tool and as a means of developing a new and better social order. I was interested in Barb's ideas and offered to fund the first year's operation of an Iowa women's law center that she would head. Barb rented an office in one of the old Dowling High School buildings on the near north side and developed a schedule of nine workshops on legal issues, the first to be held in late October. The end of her brief career in this job came on the night of her first scheduled workshop. I had invited her for dinner beforehand and she arrived in my apartment drunk and with her young son in tow. While we sat at the dinner table she told me the story of her life and all the disadvantages she had faced. She accompanied this recital with copious tears of self-pity. I felt sorry for her son, whom she seemed to ignore and who was obviously anxious for her affection. It was evident that Barb was in no condition to conduct a workshop that night. I went with her to Wilkie House where the meeting was to take place and was relieved to find that no one had showed up for the program. It turned out that Barb had a serious drinking problem that kept her from directing the law center and she soon left town. The idea of the women's law center was a good one that died at birth. Since that time I had heard that Barb was in Japan teaching martial arts so I was surprised when she called me recently from Corvalis, Oregon, ostensibly to report on Sally Hacker's health, but also to let me know that she had not had a drink in eight years.

During 1973 I worked with NOW's task force on sexism in education, investigating the extent of discrimination against girls and women in the Des Moines public school system. We ran up against stonewalling by school officials who ignored our requests for information. However, it was easy to collect enough material to enable us to file charges of sex discrimination under Title IX of the federal Higher Education Act of 1972 with the Department of Health, Education, and Welfare (HEW). Some of our information was from junior high and high school girls who had come to us with a variety of complaints about unjust treatment. Roosevelt High School students, for example, told us that after they had written a letter to the Board of Education pointing out the inequity of so-called "career" education programs—home economics for girls and shop for boys—school authorities were so threatened that they asked each complainant to bring a parent to school for individual conferences. Girls from other schools complained about lack of access to athletic facilities, such as having to use the school track at six in the morning so that the boys could have it at a more convenient time. We found that more than eight times as much money was being spent on boys' as on girls' athletics in the Des Moines school system. We also found that the small number of women in administrative positions in the school system was shrinking instead of increasing, and that there was obvious indifference to implementing an affirmative action plan. At first I had difficulty accepting the feminist insistence on greater athletic opportunities for girls. My good friend, Paula Brown, had worked for years in a futile effort to deemphasize athletics in the schools. She felt that athletics were being stressed at the expense of academic programs. I was in sympathy with Paula's mission. It seemed to me that perhaps it would be better to diminish the emphasis on boys' athletics rather than increase support for girls' sports. I soon came to realize, however, that this was an impractical approach and that denying girls opportunities for full participation in sports reinforces the concept of females as the submissive and weaker sex and helps keep us on the sidelines as mere cheerleaders.

It took four years for HEW to reply to our charges of sex discrimination in the Des Moines schools and when they did it was evident that they had done literally nothing to investigate their validity. HEW's findings, based on a superficial self-evaluation made by the Des Moines school system, found discrimination against girls in such peripheral activities as father-daughter banquets and girls' glee clubs, while completely ignoring our figures showing obvious discrimination in employment, a basic economic issue for women. NOW was furious at this unwarranted whitewash of the Des Moines school system and I tried unsuccessfully to push the ICLU into asking for a judicial review of the HEW findings. At this point, however, the legal staff of the ICLU just didn't seem interested. Although I know of no recent report on the status of sex equality in the Des Moines schools I am told that currently the athletic situation is a good deal better than in 1973, but that the percentage of women in administrative capacities is probably even lower than it was at that time. For example, during the current year, 1988–1989, in our Des Moines secondary schools, there are only ten female vice principals out of a total of thirty, and only three female principals out of a total of seventeen, none of whom head a high school.

For many feminists who found NOW too radical, the Iowa Women's Political Caucus was a more conventional type of organization with which to be associated. Instead of NOW's often flamboyant consciousness-raising tactics, the Caucus concentrated on more conventional types of political action along with the endorsement of candidates for public office. I was a charter member of the Caucus when it was organized under the leadership of Roxanne Conlin in 1973 and one of the conveners of its first convention. Although both the Caucus and NOW were filling a need in the feminist agenda, I found NOW's program more challenging and more fulfilling. So although I have always been supportive, I have never become an active Caucus member.

My involvement with party politics has been minimal although I am an avowed Democrat who attends party caucuses and gives financial support both to the party and to selected candidates, especially women who are running for public office. In the 1960s and 1970s I was a delegate to several county and state conventions but I am no longer interested in attending these conventions. They often last until the small hours of the morning and I just can't stay up that late. (I call this practice discrimination against the elderly.) One of my most memorable political activities involved supporting Shirley Chisholm, a black member of Congress, when she announced in 1971 that she was a candidate for president of the United States. I became co-chair of an Iowa committee for Chisholm with Edna Griffin, a black civil rights advocate. We opened our campaign with a press conference held in the middle of the black district in Des Moines on a wind-swept abandoned gas station lot. We never seriously expected Chisholm to achieve her goal but we wanted to demonstrate support for her by Iowa women. Our principal aim was to gather enough strength to be able to send Roxanne Conlin as a Chisholm delegate to the national Democratic convention, but we couldn't garner enough votes at the state Democratic convention to achieve our goal.

In 1980 there was a referendum in Iowa on the question of adding an equal rights amendment to the state constitution. A broad spectrum of women's groups supported this effort and many men spoke out in its favor. I gave substantial financial support to this effort and represented NOW at a hearing before the General Assembly but most of the hard work of campaigning was done by other women. In fact, I was so sanguine about the success of this referendum that I was apprehensive about its enforcement. I knew that having a law calling for equality was not enough and that continued pressure was needed to make that law effective. I needn't have worried. When the voting was over, the amendment failed by a large margin. I am of the opinion that many of the men who said they favored an equal rights amendment actually voted against it in the secrecy of the voting booth.

My activities in support of reproductive rights for women, which began when I was president of the ICLU, have continued unabated. For several years I was part of a group that organized pro-choice demonstrations on the steps of the state capitol on the anniversary of the Supreme Court decision legalizing abortion. These demonstrations were to counteract anti-abortion meetings that were held in the House chamber that same night. After our demonstration in 1980, I went up to the House chamber to hear what the opposition was saying. The speaker was a priest telling the audience that abortion was comparable to the Holocaust. This is an argument that I find demeaning to all Jews, especially the grandparents, parents, and children murdered by Hitler. Were not each of these people worth more than a day-old embryo? I subsequently sent a letter to Bishop Dingman of Des Moines telling him of my concern about this line of thinking. Granting that we would not agree on the basic issue of abortion, I hoped he would ask his priests to stop using the Holocaust argument. A gracious reply from the bishop suggested we might meet and discuss the issue. I did not follow up on his suggestion because I felt I had already conveyed my message. Instead, I called my rabbi at Temple B'Nai Jeshurun and suggested that he talk to the bishop about the matter. In 1978 I joined a picket line outside Babe's restaurant in downtown Des Moines where an anti-abortion meeting was being held. No longer did street demonstrations frighten me.

Whenever I attend my precinct caucus I introduce a pro-choice resolution. Since my precinct is located in a heavily Italian-Catholic district, pro-choice resolutions always bring forth a lot of opposition and they usually lose, although sometimes by a surprisingly small margin. One year Jim Sarcone, the perennial chair of the meeting, got so involved with arguing against my resolution that I finally took over the microphone and asked for a vote. With Sarcone counting raised hands, the result was a tie which he broke with his negative vote. Even though the resolution was defeated, I considered it a victory for our side since I think another chair would probably have counted differently.

No account of my feminist activities would be complete without some mention of the many letters I have written to all manner of people and institutions calling attention to injustices suffered by

women. My first letter about a feminist issue was published in the
Des Moines Register in October 1969. I took the paper to task for saying that the prohibition against discrimination in employment because of sex in Title VII of the Civil Rights Act of 1964 should not be
taken seriously. The paper had pointed out that the inclusion of sex
in this legislation was a fluke because it had been introduced in the
first place only as a parliamentary move to defeat the entire bill.
"Your editorial implies," I wrote, "that because women are protected
under the equal opportunity law by virtue of the support of opponents of civil rights that Title VII is still a matter for jest." The real
joke, I said, was that this provision had come to be taken seriously by
both the EEOC and the courts and it was time for the Des Moines Register to take it seriously too. This letter was the beginning of a flow of
correspondence that continues to the present day. Why didn't the
Foreign Policy Association have any women in its local branch? Why
didn't the International League for the Rights of Man change its
name? Why should I support a mikvah (ritual bath to cleanse women
after their periods) through my contribution to the United Jewish Appeal? Why didn't Wilhelmina Holladay, founder of the National Museum of Women and the Arts, stop telling reporters that she wasn't a
feminist? How many women and minorities did Sen. John Culver
have on his staff? Why did Grinnell College give its female graduates
calendars to attach to men's watchbands? Why did the Embassy Club
plan a men's grill in its new clubrooms? Why did the Des Moines Register print an obituary with the sexist heading, "Ex-publisher's Wife
Dies?" Why did the Des Moines Pioneer Club exclude women?
Weren't our foremothers pioneers too? My latest letter written in
September 1988 to George Drake, Grinnell College president, asks
why only 18 women are listed among the 102 persons whom the college claims as "distinguished alumni."

In 1981 I was inducted into the Iowa Women's Hall of Fame, an
institution founded in 1975 by the Iowa Commission on the Status of
Women. I have mixed feelings about this honor. On the one hand it
recognizes women—both living and deceased—who have contributed to the well-being of Iowa and singles them out as role models for
other women; on the other hand, to honor females separately from
males tends to indicate that women's achievements are somehow
different, that is, lesser than those of men. In my remarks following
presentation of the award by Governor Robert Ray, I said:

> I deeply appreciate this honor that you have bestowed on me today,
> and I shall cherish it. However, I cannot accept it without expressing

regret that we women have to bolster our egos by establishing our own hall of fame. When women earn $1 for every $1 men earn instead of 59 cents; when women occupy 50 percent of the seats in the Iowa Legislature instead of 11 percent; when the governor who so graciously hands out these awards is as likely to be a woman as a man, then the time will have come when we can do away with a women's hall of fame and we can compete on even terms with all Iowans for the honors of the state.

We have a lot work ahead of us before we achieve this utopia. The going will be rough, but we have no choice but to keep on struggling. Like our foremothers who fought so long and hard for the right to vote, we won't stop until the job is done.

These remarks were met with a standing ovation. They were also published on the editorial page of the *Des Moines Register*. A few days later when a stranger stopped me in the grocery store to tell me that she had put that newspaper clipping on her refrigerator door I felt that I had really become a person of importance.

9

COLLECTING ART BY WOMEN

My feminist interests and my interest in art found common ground in the 1960s when I became active in collecting art by women. My first purchase of a work of art by a woman was made in 1964. This was an oil titled "Women Walking," by the American artist, Isabel Bishop. At this time I was immersed in research for my book on the history of woman suffrage in Iowa and I was becoming increasingly aware of the difficulties women face in our society. The Bishop oil, appropriately, was purchased with funds from the bequest of my mother who had died four years before. Although I did not limit my collecting to works by females for at least another ten years, the Bishop was actually the beginning of my collection of art by women. When the Bishop painting was hung in the place of honor over our living room sofa, Maurie noticed that it was not signed. Although I had purchased the picture from Bishop's dealer, I subsequently wrote Bishop directly asking whether or not she customarily signed her works. I received a very cordial letter in reply asking if she could "stop by" Des Moines some day and sign the picture. (Actually, she ended up signing the picture in New York when I loaned it to a retrospective exhibition of her work.) At Bishop's suggestion, I also called her the next time I was in New York. She welcomed me warmly, taking me to lunch and showing me her studio on Union Square. She also gave me an etching that she had made in preparation for my painting. On my later trips to New York, Isabel entertained me in her lovely home in the Riverdale section. Isabel Bishop died in 1988 after a long illness. She was a sensitive, caring person and I feel privileged to have known her.

My art collecting began when my mother purchased that oil painting for my thirteenth-birthday present and continued through my high school years when she purchased prints for me. The first purchases that I myself made were while I was in graduate school. At this time I acquired a beautiful gouache by the nineteenth century French artist, Camille Pissarro; a gouache by the contemporary Italian artist, Emanuele Romano; and a miscellany of prints and drawings ranging from fifteenth-century German woodcuts to nineteenth-century lithographs by the French artist, Honoré Daumier. For a number of years after my marriage in 1938 I virtually ceased collecting art. My interest in collecting was renewed during Dwight Kirsch's tenure as director of the Art Center from 1950 to 1958 (It was he who interested me in the work of Isabel Bishop); but by far the most influential person in helping me build my collection has been Jim Demetrion, director of the Art Center from 1969 to 1984. Jim, who has become a good friend, has continued to advise me since becoming director of the Hirschhorn Museum in Washington, D.C. With the exception of works by women artists in my collection, many of the works of art that I have acquired over the years have been given away. Art Center records show that between 1948 and 1987 I gave more than sixty works of art to this institution alone. They range from a page of a fifteenth-century illuminated manuscript, to the Pissarro gouache, a George Grosz watercolor, and important contemporary prints by Claes Oldenburg and Jasper Johns. I have also given works of art to the Art Museum of the University of Iowa and to Grinnell College, Cornell College, Simpson College, Drake University, and the Hirschhorn Museum. A few of my treasures have been given to personal friends. I don't want to belittle my charitable impulses, but I am beginning to wonder if my gifts were motivated, in part at least, by an ambivalence about collecting stemming from Mother's pressure on me to become a collector.

My purchase of the Bishop oil in 1964 was followed two years later by the acquisition of two more works by women; a watercolor by the American artist, Marguerite Zorach and a woodcut by the German artist, Käthe Kollwitz. In 1971 I purchased a print by the German artist, Paula Modersohn Becker, from a "collector's choice" exhibition at the Art Center which Jim Demetrion had curated. It was not until 1976, however, that I made another major purchase of a work of art by a woman. This was a 1909 oil titled "Fishers" by the Russian avant-garde artist, Natalia Gontcharova. This picture depicts peasants fishing with a net in a pond surrounded by trees. It shows the influence of both Gauguin and the Fauves, yet it is distinctly Russian in feeling and could never be mistaken for the work of a French artist. I had not heard of Gontcharova until one day at the Art Center when Jim Demetrion suggested that I go down to the storeroom and look at this painting that was for sale by a California collector. "It is even painted by a woman," he said. That was all the bait I needed. I took one look at the painting and was overwhelmed by its beauty. I went back to Jim's office and told him that I wasn't going to worry about how I was going to pay for this painting—it was more than I had ever before paid for a work of art—I was only going to worry about where to hang it. There was no trouble finding space for it in my living room and it has been hanging there ever since. With the purchase of the Gontcharova painting I became interested in the Russian avant-garde (c. 1905–1925) and found that there were an unusual number of very fine women artists active in this movement. This interest has led to the purchase of works by other Russian avant-garde women—names as yet little known in this country—such as Olga Rozanova, Nina Kogan, Alexandra Exter, Nadezhda Udaltsova, and Liubov Popova. Seeking out the works of these women has been an exciting quest but also a frustrating one because I would like to know more about them and there is so little information. (Until the present perestroika, their work has been out of favor in Russia.) At the present time there are several scholars working in this area. I have recently gotten in touch with a Yale student who has chosen Gontcharova as the subject for her doctoral thesis. She promises to send me a copy as soon as it is completed.

Another artist who is just now becoming of interest to scholars is a German woman, Hannah Höch, who is best known for having been a member of the Berlin Dada group in the early 1920s. I first became aware of Höch when I saw one of her Dada collages in an exhibition in Berlin in 1977 and thought it a very interesting piece. The following year I purchased a Höch watercolor and later I acquired four of her collages and an oil painting. The oil painting, "Der Weg" (The Way), painted in 1927, is a magnificent work. It shows a procession winding down from the upper-left corner to the lower-right corner of the picture. This procession, much of it enigmatic, is intended to be symbolic of Höch's life. In the upper part is a bucolic scene with two naked figures—Adam and Eve?—and a small child walking ahead of them. Then comes a procession of animals and birds, including a giraffe and elephant. Next in line is a graveyard and a funeral procession, and then a group of fantastic animals similar to those painted by the fifteenth-century Flemish artist, Hieronymus Bosch. Next, stepping off to one side of the procession, is a male figure painted in blue—possibly Höch's current lover—followed by two female figures, one of whom is pregnant, and two small children holding hands. Höch is said to have had an abortion in the 1920s and this picture seems to represent her trauma over this event. I am waiting for scholars, who are currently doing research on Höch, to help decode all the symbols in this fascinating painting. Meanwhile, it is a constant challenge to try to decipher it myself.

Other works in my collection include a self-portrait by the Mexican artist, Frida Kahlo, and a winter scene by the German artist, Gabriele Munter. Among the American artists represented in my collection are Eva Hesse, Lee Krasner, Dorothea Tanning, Agnes Martin, and Agnes Pelton. The primary purpose of my collecting is to gather a limited number of works that make a strong feminist statement about the quality of art produced by women. I do not aim to be historically inclusive, but I try to find works that can hold their own in any company. The works of the early twentieth-century avant-garde women are of particular interest to me, but my collection also contains a wide variety of works by other women. I have no works earlier than 1900 with the exception of two prints by French artists: a drypoint by Berthe Morisot executed about 1890, and an 1895 soft-ground etching by Suzanne Valadon. My collecting is limited to so-called "fine art" as traditionally defined. I have not attempted to include crafts such as quilts, weaving, and pottery, which in many cultures are considered women's special province. Although there are good arguments for redefining fine art in terms including crafts, I have chosen not to do so.

It is not unusual for people to challenge me for limiting my collecting of works of art to those by women. "Aren't women artists given their fair share of recognition these days?" I am asked. Or, "What have women artists done that merits special recognition?" My answer to the first question is that although women have made great gains in the past few years, there is still a long way to go. In fact, the feminist artist, Nancy Spero, stated in 1987 that it can be argued that the art world is not any more open to women artists today than it was in 1969–1970 when women made their first forays against the art establishment.* The second question implies that the bringing together of art by women is a futile occupation resulting in a second-rate collection. This question is best answered by the quality of the art I have

*Jeanne Siegel, "Nancy Spero: Woman as Protagonist," Arts, September 1987, p. 3.

collected. I like to recall the visit of Ulfert Wilke, former director of the University of Iowa Art Museum, who came to see my collection several years ago. "Why, these paintings are good!" he remarked with great surprise. Or more recently, when I talked with the art insurance mogul, Huntington Block, in Washington, D.C., about insuring my collection of art by women, his first comment was to the effect that he didn't approve of this kind of collection. Then he looked at the list of works which I own and he said, "Any museum in the country would be delighted to have a collection of this quality." This kind of reaction reassures me that I am not going amiss in the direction of my collecting.

Not all women, however, approve of this type of segregation and I can understand their concern. For women to be segregated usually means they are not as good as males doing the same kind of work. Yet until women are treated as equals in our society, I think a collection of the kind I am putting together has a valid statement to make about the quality of women's work. Dorothea Tanning is one artist whose work I own who would not be happy to be represented in my collection. Despite the fact that she met her husband, Max Ernst, in 1942 when he came to select one of her paintings for a women's exhibition, she has since become adamantly opposed to showing with other women. In response to an invitation to lend a work to an exhibition of avant-garde women artists which was shown in Milan, Italy, in 1980, Tanning not only refused to lend anything but also suggested that each woman represented in the show should have a physical examination to be sure that she wasn't a man in disguise. She added that she regretted that works of hers over which she has no control are occasionally shown in women's exhibitions. The organizers of the Milan exhibition published Tanning's letter of refusal in the exhibition catalog. Tanning in her memoirs does admit that she feels "a little something" about women's inferior status but that there is nothing to be done about the situation of women short of revamping the whole human race.* My feeling is that although revamping the human race is a tough job we had better start now if we ever want to do something about it.

Having gathered a group of works by women artists I have to ask, do these works indicate a unique woman's sensibility? My answer is no. For the most part, as Tamar Garb points out, it would be a mistake to create a common identity for female artists.† Each artist relates in her own specific way to the artistic and political debates of her time;

*Dorothea Tanning, *Birthday*, San Francisco: Lapis Press, 1986, 177.
†Tamar Garb, *Women Impressionists*, New York: Rizzoli Press, 1986, 5.

and the strongest intellectual and aesthetic collaborations women develop are with their male colleagues rather than among themselves. Nevertheless, the conditions under which women live are different from those of their male colleagues and, to a certain extent, their social and psychological situation accounts for the work they produce. Some of the works in my collection seem to stem from a female perspective. Tanning's splendid drawing, "Musical Chairs," depicting a girl tumbling off her chair into a soft mass of cloud-like material in which she is about to disappear, seems to relate to the uncertainties women face in their lives. Höch's "Der Weg" certainly stems from her feelings of frustrated maternity. Suzanne Valadon's print depicting a nubile young woman is drawn with abrupt, edgy, hard lines and lacks the sensuous eroticism of her mentor, Edgar Degas. Valadon, in this way, rejects the nude's usual signification as a sexual object to be enjoyed by the male viewer. On the other hand, many, if not most of the works in my collection give no indication of the gender of the artist who produced them.

I like to tell people facetiously that I can collect art because I have my mother's permission. But as I write, I wonder if there isn't something more. Does my collecting of works by women represent a kind of reconciliation with my mother? I no longer have an impulse to give these works away but want to keep them intact as a collection that I plan someday to give to a museum. Perhaps I have finally lost most of my ambivalence about collecting and can now accept Mother's influence without feelings of rejection or resentment. In any event, writing these memoirs has certainly made me see my mother more clearly and helped me come to terms with what she has meant in my life. It has been a long, rough road to travel but in the end the journey has been worthwhile.

INDEX